Literature Support is an occasional series of shorter books designed to guide teachers within particular areas of children's literature. Each book suggests ways of approaching one of these areas in the classroom and includes extended lists of relevant titles.

Literature Support Series

Quest for Wonders

MYTHS AND LEGENDS IN THE CLASSROOM

John Tingay

Illustrated by Kim Gamble

PRIMARY ENGLISH TEACHING ASSOCIATION

National Library of Australia Cataloguing-in-publication data

Tingay, John
Quest for wonders: myths and legends in the classroom

Bibliography
ISBN 1 875622 05 5

1. Folk literature – Study and teaching (Primary). 2. Folklore and education. 3. Reading (Primary). 4. Education, Primary – Activity programs. I. Primary English Teaching Association (Australia). II. Title. (Series: Literature support series).

372.64044

First published June 1993
Copyright © Primary English Teaching Association 1993
Laura Street Newtown NSW 2042 Australia
Cover design by Kim Gamble
Designed by Anne-Marie Rahilly and Jeremy Steele
Edited by Jeremy Steele
Typeset in 9.5/13 Stone Serif at the T & D Centre
Cnr The Boulevarde and Toothill Street Lewisham NSW 2049
Printed by Ambassador Press
51 Good Street Granville NSW 2142

Contents

Introduction	1
1 What Are Myths and Legends?	3
2 What Are Myths and Legends about?	12
3 The Classroom Audience	28
4 What Next?	38
Select Bibliography	55
Books for the Teacher	56
General Mythology	57
Greek Mythology	59
Northern European Mythology	63
Australian Aboriginal Lore	67
Myths and Legends of Other Peoples	72

Acknowledgements

I would like to acknowledge important help and encouragement which I have received from several people whilst putting this book together. My wife, Heather, has been an invaluable encourager, adviser and patient co-worker, particularly in the Greek myths and legends section. Jeremy Steele and Vivienne Nicoll-Hatton have been a highly professional team at PETA, and their wisdom and guidance, especially on the Perth to Sydney telephone lines, have been most supportive. Finally, I should like to thank my colleagues and students in the Department of Language Arts Education at Edith Cowan University, who have been a valuable sounding board for ideas.

J. T.

Introduction

In Shakespeare's *A Midsummer Night's Dream*, when Bottom the Weaver says 'I am to discourse wonders', he is thinking of the play which he and his friends are about to perform for the Athenian aristocracy. However, his words could well be applied to the stories, originally passed on by word of mouth, which are the subject of this book.

To children in primary schools, myths and legends are wonders principally because they are good stories. They have excitement and intrigue, they tell of bravery and heroism. They take the listener or reader into fantastic worlds, beyond the usual scope of literary experiences — worlds in which magical and strange feats occur; worlds of superhuman dimensions to which the wide-ranging imaginations of primary school children can readily respond.

Yet though these qualities are often enough in themselves to satisfy children in the classroom, myths and legends from many cultures around the world have other qualities which would justify the word 'wonders'. Almost always they have deeper layers of meaning which are related to important concerns in the societies they derive from, and which continue to resonate today. They deal with matters of life and death, with loves and enmities. In a culture like ours, which puts a premium on immediate experience, they help children to realise that people who lived in remote countries hundreds — even thousands — of years ago were moved by feelings and motives they can recognise in themselves. In a culture which also sets a high value on scientific rationalism, they admit children to an enormous fund of human experience mediated by the poetic imagination (which for most of us is at its most powerful in childhood).

Mythologies have proved to be an almost inexhaustible source of inspiration to the artistic talents of successive generations. Since the Renaissance countless painters have borrowed subjects from Greek myths and legends, and one can get a sudden sense of their continuing fertility of suggestion across different artistic realms in coming upon Brueghel's painting of *The Fall of Icarus* celebrated in Auden's poem 'Musée des Beaux Arts' some four hundred years later. Opera has drawn on Greek themes from its inception (Monteverdi's *Orfeo*) down to our own times (Tippett's *King Priam*). Playwrights like Racine and Cocteau have used Greek myths and legends as the basis for part of their creative output. Wagner in music and Tolkien in literature were deeply indebted to Norse mythology, and the Arthurian legends have even spawned a musical. D. H. Lawrence, too, was affected by the Aztec myths about Quetzalcoatl.

Myths and legends have been a vital element in the expression of human culture for thousands of years, and until societies acquired a literary base, they were orally transmitted from one generation to the next. Today, however, with our vast array of written texts available on paper and disk, we tend not value the oral text as highly as our ancestors did. This book seeks to give a valid place to the oral literature tradition. Myths and legends can become an integral part of our classrooms and strengthen the oracy values we espouse. Teachers can move from story reading into storytelling and use myths and legends as the basis for this and other classroom activities.

The text that follows is divided into four chapters and concludes with a bibliography. The first two chapters describe the nature and scope of myths and legends, giving examples of stories that can be used in the classroom. The third chapter discusses how myths and legends can best be shared with children, while the fourth suggests a variety of activities which can be prompted by retellings and readings. The bibliography gives extensive lists of source books and reference books for different mythologies, as well as books for the teacher.

~ CHAPTER ONE ~

WHAT ARE MYTHS AND LEGENDS?

There are many people today who talk about 'myths' when it's quite obvious that they do not mean traditional stories. For them the word implies an untrue story, and it's often used to dismiss a claim by a political opponent. Similarly, the word 'legend' is often applied to people still alive who have achieved glory in sport or some other pursuit. (The phrase 'a legend in his/her own lifetime' refers more to the person than the stories about him or her.) These contemporary uses of 'myth' and 'legend' are perfectly legitimate of course, but they are extensions of the original cores of meaning which concern us when thinking of stories which can be used in the classroom.

Most of the stories characterised as myths and legends in the classroom had currency long before their 'authors' began to write. They were developed in oral traditions of storytelling which may have lasted for centuries before the stories were written down. They are usually about gods and heroes, about the beginnings of the civilisations which first told them, and had special significance in the lives and faiths of the storytellers. They come from cultures which have long since ceased to exist, as well as from contemporary societies. There may be great differences between the myths and legends of one culture and another, and even different versions of the same myth within the one culture. Nevertheless there are characteristics which are common to myths and legends from different cultures.

Although it's not easy to be definitive about what distinguishes myths and legends, for my purposes as a teacher I find it helpful to work with this simple definition:

> *Myths are stories about gods and other immortal, supernatural beings (including animals), who are involved in creation and other non-human acts; legends tell of the exploits of heroes, who are usually partly immortal and partly mortal.*

This definition enables us to separate myths and legends from folktales, which are stories about ordinary human beings rather than people with divine status. (In this context, it's interesting to note that the word 'legend' was first used in mediaeval times to refer to accounts of the lives of saints.) Characters in folktales may complete unusual or difficult exploits, but they succeed not because of their partial divinity but because of their humanity. Admittedly there are groups of folktales containing supernatural elements — giants, witches, fairy godmothers and so on — some of which resemble the immortal elements found in myths. Yet though the giant in 'Jack and the Beanstalk' may be like the giants of Jotunheim, he behaves like an excessively large man, and he is certainly not immortal. Indeed there is often more realism in folktales, even where the supernatural is concerned — just as the fairies in *A Midsummer Night's Dream* show human foibles: 'Lord, what fools these mortals be' may be applied to all of the characters, whether human or fairy.

The bulk of writing about myths and legends has tended to concentrate on non-literary matters. The stories have often been regarded as simple narratives, the main interest lying in their *interpretation* as myths and legends. If teachers go to the library in search of copies of these stories, they will find little in the literature section, but will see them on the shelves devoted to religion, philosophy, psychology and social sciences. This is all very well, but it tends to detract from the value of the stories in schools. Myths and legends are almost entirely good stories which children can enjoy as such.

Most of the myths and legends available to us have come from classical Greece and from Norse and Celtic mythology. Over the past few years myths and legends from Aboriginal Australians have become more widely known, and stories from other parts of the world which reflect the current ethnic composition of Australia have also gained an audience.

Myths and legends are oral literature

I believe that the most important characteristic of myths and legends is their common tradition of oral transmission. These were stories told by the old to the young, passed on from one generation to the next. In some cultures, such as the Norse or ancient Greek, the poet or minstrel recorded the deeds of heroes and related stories about the gods, often those from whom the heroes were descended. The teller of these stories was an important person, respected and valued in society, although we should recognise him as a *reteller* of the stories, not necessarily as an author.

One of the best places to get a feel for all of this is Book 8 of the *Odyssey*, which introduces us to Demodocus, the poet at the Phaeacian court. He is distinguished not only by his genius but by blindness (Homer is reputed to have been blind too), and the herald takes special care of him and the lyre he uses to accompany his declamation. His silver-studded chair is placed centrally in the banqueting hall, and he is always treated with particular honour. Twice in the hall he recounts episodes from the recently concluded Trojan war (to the satisfaction of Odysseus, who praises him extravagantly), and although these are sketched in sparse outline, we still get a sense of legends in the making. In between these two performances, when he is called on to play for dancers in the open air, he modulates into a song about the celestial affair between Ares and Aphrodite. Unlike the Trojan war episodes, this story is given in considerable detail, and with inescapable humour. Though skilfully blended into the text of the *Odyssey*, it is sufficiently well developed to stand on its own — indeed, it may well have done so.

We can also see the importance of the story reteller in the folk song 'The Minstrel Boy', in which the minstrel boy goes to war, never to return. His loss is mourned because his retelling of the deeds of heroes will not be heard again. He is described as 'the warrior bard', a poet and storyteller of importance to the oral tradition. 'The Minstrel Boy' is a very recent folk song when measured against the centuries of storytelling that preceded it, but it is typical of the tradition of storytelling.

The oral tradition started before writing in a given language developed and continued alongside writing, at least long enough for the oral stories to be written down and so be transferred to a literary tradition. Much of the nature of these stories arose from the practice of oral transmission. In storytelling societies the myths and legends were well known. Homer could safely assume that his audience would amplify Demodocus' allusions to the Trojan war. Frequently the interest of the hearers was as much in the application of stories to the occasion of the retelling as in the stories themselves: on the night before a battle Viking warriors would listen to stories of previous

victories and the valour of their chief, and of a cycle of successes all the way back to an ancestor destined to march triumphantly out of Valhalla to fight at Ragnarok. Thus it's not surprising that the written versions which we have are often unelaborated. The writer would simply give the outline of a story, enough to remind contemporary readers (there were probably few enough of these anyway) of a story which they had heard in elaborated form many times before.

What we have today are written versions of these spoken or sung stories rather than the sort of stories *we* would write, which are usually intended for the reader rather than the listener. Of course there are novels, such as *The King Must Die* (Mary Renault) or *Dragon Slayer* (Rosemary Sutcliff), which draw on material from myth and legend but are written in a literary form. But if we sit down to read a collection of myths and legends, they may appear to be simple, even childish stories. Written down, they can easily lose the drama and nuances of an oral retelling. The tone of voice, facial expressions and gestures of the storyteller are lost; there is no musical accompaniment, no interaction with an audience. G. S. Kirk (1975), commenting on *Tanglewood Tales* (Hawthorne's retelling of Greek myths) describes them as 'spare, simple, slightly emotional and intended for children'. 'Unfortunately,' he adds, 'they can *only* satisfy children or the childlike'. However, this apparent criticism should be regarded as part of the strength of myths and legends. Many of the written versions available today consist of the bare bones of the story. They are simple and usually unadorned; elaboration is left for the contemporary storyteller to add as felt appropriate for the audience, just as the poet, minstrel and storyteller of old did.

When literate societies began to write down stories contained in the myths and legends of different peoples, the stories tended to become relatively fixed. It seems probable that until that point they changed over time to reflect several different matters, such as regional variations within the cult of a god or goddess. In some cultures there are different versions of a traditional story which seem to indicate that at least two parallel yet distinct versions coexisted at the time when the story was first written down (the two juxtaposed accounts of the creation of the world at the beginning of Genesis are a case in point). Many anthropologists and scholars from other disciplines have argued over which is the 'authentic' version; this may well be a valid academic pursuit, but it only underlines the nature of an oral tradition. Rather like the party game 'Chinese Whispers', every time a story is passed on in this way, it may change according to the perceptions of the listeners and the context of the retelling. But, unlike 'Chinese Whispers', the retelling of myths and legends always retained a credible story. The retellers produced different versions because they told the stories to different audiences. Nowadays members of storytellers guilds in Australia quite unashamedly change stories so that they become the reteller's own. Even the same story retold by one person may change every time it is told. This is a practice not far removed from that of the original tellers of myths and legends.

It was quite common in many societies for a retelling to emphasise a link between the audience, patron or chief on the one hand, and the hero of the story on the other. Some of the records of Greek myths, for example, come from the choral songs of Pindar (and others like him), in which he eulogised a member of a distinguished family who had won a victory at one of the Greek games. He would set the victory in a context of allusion to gods or heroes which reflected glory back to the victor, his family or the district from which he came. In such a context stories could be 'slightly adapted' to fit the occasion — reminding us, incidentally, that variation is perfectly possible even after stories have been wholly or partly absorbed into a written tradition.

'Purposes' of myths and legends

While myths from different cultures around the world have similar origins as traditional stories passed on by oral transmission, there are also resemblances in the stories and beings involved. For example, the three Fates in Greek mythology and their 'sisters' in Norse mythology, the Norns, are very similar: they are depicted as spinners, measurers and cutters of the thread of life. Both groups signify that when your life-span, allotted by an external and 'divine' order, has reached its end, then you die. This is an example of a *function* of mythology: in addition to being good tales, myths and legends explain things which the society feels are important. These are the truths of myths and legends — they dramatise and interpret aspects of the human condition and explain central beliefs for the societies which create them. To ask 'Did it really happen?' is an irrelevance. The truth of myths and legends lies at this poetic, interpretative level, and to contrast myth and reality is a product of a nineteenth-century western viewpoint.

Myths and nature

There are a number of theories to account for the creation of myths and legends. It has been suggested that some explain or at least refer to the origins of the earth, stars, weather and other natural phenomena. For example, lightning and the hurling of thunderbolts was what Zeus (Jupiter to the Romans) resorted to when he was displeased — so did Thor. Mortals then had to placate him with sacrifices. In Sumerian mythology Enlil was the 'lord of the air and the winds' and, like many gods of different peoples, a powerful weather god. Water held a fascination for myth and legend makers. Many societies had their gods of the oceans, such as Poseidon for the Greeks, as well as deities for rivers, springs, mountains and other

geographical features. If a spring dried up, it was a sign that the appropriate deity was angry with mortals.

Many significant 'nature' myths are concerned with animals. Animals appear in myths from nearly all cultures. The ancient Egyptians worshipped gods in animal form for several thousand years: Horus was a hawk and Anubis a jackal. The feathered serpent, Quetzalcoatl, is prominent in Mexican mythology, and the rainbow serpent, Julunggul, is seen by Australian Aborigines as a creator-god and bringer of civilisation.

'Just so' myths and legends

Some myths are believed to offer reasons for the existence or causes of certain features of the real world. For Hesiod, an early Greek poet, the origin of fire was explained by the myth of Prometheus stealing it from Zeus. I find the Kipling term 'just so' a convenient way of referring to this kind of story. In Kipling's *Just So Stories* the emphasis is on *how* something occurred, such as how the camel got its hump. More recently Ted Hughes has written a similar set of stories (*How the Whale Became*). Many published Australian Aboriginal myths are of this sort. Why are there black patches of land near Daly River? Why do dogs eat their food raw? The answers to these questions are explained in the story about Chicken Hawk, Big Hawk and Dog.

Customs and institutions

Some myths and legends seem to have a relationship to a custom or institution that confirms it for people in a traditional society. A group ritual may often have a myth to explain its origin and purpose. In some Australian Aboriginal societies certain myths may have their significance explained in an initiation ceremony. Oodgeroo Noonuccal points out that some Aboriginal myths and legends are told as cautionary tales to instil respect for the tribal system. This kind of myth is almost absent from some cultures (such as the Norse) but present in others. For example, the Greeks in classical times sacrificed to the gods only the inedible parts of an animal, a custom explained in the myth Hesiod gives about Prometheus offering Zeus a choice of meat or bones. Zeus chose the bones which Prometheus had covered with fat to make them look like meat.

Myths with creative powers

Some myths appear to be retold in order to re-establish a creative era. Each year the Greeks told the myth of how Demeter found her daughter Persephone and brought her back from the underworld, with the result that crops began to grow again, thrusting their way out of the dark soil and into the air. The telling of the myth helped the fertility of the crops. It is a common belief among Australian Aborigines that beings which existed in the beginning still do so and influence events in the life of Aborigines today. The Dreamtime is brought into the present with potent and fruitful results.

~ CHAPTER TWO ~

WHAT ARE MYTHS AND LEGENDS ABOUT?

1 Creation and creators

The creation of the universe, the world, human beings and other living creatures is one of the major themes of most mythologies. Prominent is the idea of order arising out of a void — the word *chaos* or its equivalent usually seems to refer to a void as the source of the substances or peoples created. In a Chinese myth Pan-Ku came out of the egg-like chaos and divided the world into earth (*yin*) and heaven (*yang*). In Norse mythology the void was Ginnungagap, where the warm air from Muspelheim met the cold from Niflheim; there the ice began to thaw and the droplets of water acquired life and became Ymir, the frost giant.

The emphasis of the Hindu *Markandeya Purana* is rather different: it states that Brahma existed independently of space and time, that Askhara-Brahma first showed himself, in a world of pure ideas, as a vowel sound whose echoes and re-echoes eventually formed the world (this is similar to the beginning of the Gospel of St. John: 'In the beginning was the word . . . '). Different again is a Japanese creation myth telling how Izanagi and Izanami summoned the first land mass from the misty sea by churning it with a spear, which is not unlike the account given by a Phoenician writer:

> *In the beginning there was nothing but a dark and windy wallowing upheaval. The winds twisted themselves into a love-knot of desire. This eventually lead to a watery slime called Mot which bred living things, simple at first, but more complex later.*

In some myths animals are the creators. According to some Australian Aboriginal myths the world serpent produced the cosmos out of its own body, and in ancient Egypt the ibis-headed god Thoth, who was also the bringer of wisdom and the art of writing, was regarded as the creator who hatched the cosmic egg and by his speech called into being the original four pairs of gods and goddesses.

Many mythologies include couples believed to be the parents of humankind. Examples include Isis and Osiris in Egypt, Fu Hsi and Nu Kua in China, and Izanagi and Izanami in Japan. These last two, after creating the earth, built a hall with a pillar. Every time they stepped round the pillar and met, they greeted each other with the words 'Oh! What a handsome young man!' and 'Oh! What a lovely maiden!' After their first union a leech was born, and a small island after the second. They went on to produce much more, including the eight islands of Japan, the sea, the rest of the earth's surface, seasons, wind, trees, mountains, and finally the swift Spirit of Fire.

2 The worlds

After creation, the myth tellers began to establish a cosmography of the worlds which had been created. There were skies or heavens as well as underworlds and seas, and with each of these regions came its own deity or deities.

Arguably the most important feature of our world is the sun, for it is essential to all the life we know. In mythology the sun often has supreme power, or at least a crucial place in an array of gods. It is the giver of warmth and energy, a nurturer of life; as fire, it burns, withers and destroys; it gives light during the day and is associated with the mind and intellect; symbolically, it is considered to have a male force and is often represented by gold, the most precious of elements. The sun may be visualised as a carriage or chariot drawn across the sky each day by fiery horses; or it may be the bird-man Garuda, who carries the great Hindu god Vishnu on his back across the sky. Sun gods are often associated with a symbolic circle shape, and they include Helios, Apollo, Shamash, Savitri and Surya. In order to secure the return of the sun and ensure the sun god's goodwill, sun-worshipping peoples built altars and edifices which marked solstices, and some, such as the Dakota and Hopi Indians, had sun-dances.

The moon also features strongly in post-creation mythologies. It is sometimes linked with the sun and becomes a parallel feature or goddess. In Greek mythology, for instance, the twins Apollo and Artemis were identified with the earlier sun and moon deities, Helios and Selene (who were also related to each other). In Hindu mythology the moon god was Chandra, and the Huaztecs in Mexico would direct their prayers for love and the gift of children to their moon goddess, Tlazolteotl. An Australian Aboriginal story tells of the moon as a fat man who was drowned trying to flirt with some girls at night. As he slowly sank on his side, the shape of his round belly above the water changed like the shape of the moon changing during its cycle.

The stars too have mythical associations. The Greeks held that the Pleiades were seven virgins who were the offspring of Pleione, a sea nymph seduced by the Titan Atlas. Orion the hunter lusted after all seven at once and chased them without success for five years. Zeus thought to settle the matter by placing them and Orion in the heavens as constellations. That did not really end the chase, however; for part of the year Orion still pursues the Pleiades across the sky.

Interestingly the Pleiades and Orion star groups feature in Australian Aboriginal bark paintings, and there is a Pitjantjara story similar to the Greek myth:

> *Old Man Yoola always wanting women. One day he saw seven sisters; he chased them. To get away they flew into the sky. They came down again at the rock hole Karraloo. Old Man Yoola walked after them, slow, trailing his spear. That spear made valleys in this country. Old Man Yoola tracked the sisters all the way to the big water hole Wankarreenga. When they saw him coming they jumped in the water. Everybody drowned. Their spirits are Stars now, crossing the sky. Old Man Yoola still on the go. Sisters still saying 'No. No.'*
> (Robinson 1956)

Rainbows have significance in various myths. Aukelenuiaiko of Hawaii, a south Pacific hero, reached heaven across a rainbow bridge, and the Norse gods of Asgard crossed over another to enter or leave their kingdom. Indian and Chinese paintings of Buddha show him seated on a rainbow, just as Byzantine Christian art images Mary on one. At the end of the flood which Noah and his family survived, Jehovah placed a rainbow in the Mt Ararat sky as a symbol of the covenant between himself and all living creatures. Celtic lore held that rainbows could bestow treasure in the form of wisdom and awareness (though for years the Irish peasantry believed that leprechauns had hidden a pot of gold at the end of a rainbow).

Thunder and lightning have been widely regarded as the work of the gods. Thunder is the voice of the gods — often delivering minatory messages. Thor's chariot had noisy wheels which were believed to be the source of thunder, although his hammer, Mjollnir, was also associated with it. The god Indra defeated the serpent demon Vrita with thunder and lightning, according to the Vedas, thus releasing the pent-up monsoon clouds to water the land of India.

Concepts of heaven, paradise, hell and earth are still with us today as part of many different faiths, and parallels are to be found in many mythologies, where the separate regions have their associated gods and goddesses. When Zeus and his two brothers, Hades and Poseidon, divided up the world after the overthrow of the Titans, Hades became the god of the underworld (also called Hades) and was responsible for the souls of the dead, Poseidon (also known as 'earth-shaker') became the god of the sea, and Zeus reigned supreme on the top of Mt Olympus. Beneath the Norse world lay Niflheim, which contained Hel, the place for the departed, presided over by a monster of the same name. All people went to Hel at death except for the heroes who were killed in battle — they were taken by the Valkyries to Valhalla to while away the time until the final battle of Ragnarok.

3 Animals and part-animals

Most mythologies have animals as an integral part of their schemes, reflecting the close relationship of people and animals all over the world, respect or reverence for animal qualities such as speed, strength, cunning or fertility, and fear of the dangers wild animals might represent (including the wilder, less acceptable aspects of human behaviour). We also find creatures which occur only in mythology, such as dragons or phoenixes; regular animals with strange features, such as Cerberus, the three-headed dog of the Greek underworld, and creatures which are part-human and part-animal, such as centaurs or satyrs.

Some animals are associated with the sun (lion, bull, ram, falcon and phoenix) or with the moon (wolf, dog, snake, hare and frog). The Peruvian Indians linked the dog with the creation of the world. In some parts of the Nile basin the bull, the ram, the falcon and the cow were gods associated with creation and fertility. Better known are the part-animal Egyptian gods typified by the form of the Sphinx: Horus was a falcon-headed man and Anubis had the head of a jackal.

In Greek mythology the centaur Chiron, half-man, half-horse, was a wise creature who advised both Achilles and Heracles. However, he was unique; centaurs were usually associated with wild, violent behaviour, typified in the attempted rape of Heracles' wife, Deianara, by Nessus. The satyrs were wild and lustful too, but lazier and less threatening. Characteristically portrayed with some goat or horse features, they lived in the woods and mountains and followed Dionysus, the wine god. Their leader was Silenus (older and strictly not a satyr himself); he was fat, jovial and often too drunk to walk, but credited with prophetic powers.

Some mythological creatures are like super animals — for example, Pegasus, a winged horse captured and tamed by Bellerophon. He became a symbol of poetic genius because one of the springs of water that arose from his hoof prints was Hippocrene, which was sacred to the Muses. He was a very useful horse to have in battle as he enabled his rider to fly above enemies in relative safety and attack them with missiles.

One of the victims of Bellerephon and Pegasus was the Chimaera, a fire-breathing monster combining elements of lion, goat and serpent. The Chimaera was not unlike the dragons which appear in myths and legends from many cultures, including those of China and Japan. There, however, they are usually associated with good qualities. In China they symbolise the power of the emperor and the fertility of the earth, while a typical Japanese story reveals a creature very different from the one killed by St George.

This story tells of a young water dragon attacked by Tengu, a large firebird, in the garden of a Buddhist monastery. The dragon was too small to fight Tengu, who quickly carried him away and dropped him in the cleft of a rock to die. A monk drawing water in the garden noticed that the dragon was gone. Just then a shadow fell over him and he looked up to see Tengu. He shook his fist, but was himself picked up and dropped above the same cleft. However, he spread his sleeves out wide and 'parachuted' down to the rock. He had a little water left in his pitcher and poured it on the dragon, blessing him as he wet his head. The water caused the dragon to grow into a full-sized creature, able to break out of the rocky crevice and fly home, taking the monk on his back.

Many of the stories about animals show them behaving as humans but with a specific characteristic, rather like the animals in Aesop's fables. Thus a fox may be cunning and a snake deceitful. An Australian Aboriginal story about the Whowie, a predatory creature who grew too big for his boots, relates how he was finally disposed of by other animals forming an alliance and attacking him like a United Nations force.

4 Gifts and skills

Fire is an essential tool for mankind. In mythology its importance is enshrined in stories about how mankind came to have fire, and in fire deities. The Greek myth of the theft of fire from Zeus has already been mentioned: Prometheus stole a spark hidden in a stalk of fennel and so distributed fire to humans. Zeus punished him by chaining him to Mt Caucasus, where an eagle ate his liver each day (being immortal, it grew back each night). He was finally released by Heracles.

In north-west Peru the Jivaro Indians believed that the first man to make fire was Takkea. Birds tried to steal it, but he crushed them between the door and the doorpost as they flew into his house. He lived on roast bird. However, Takkea's wife took pity on the hummingbird, Himbui, who was fluttering helplessly along the path to the house. She brought him in to warm himself, but when her back was turned he dipped his tail feathers into the fire and flew away. Then he set alight the bark of a tree and called upon the rest of creation to share the fire.

The Djuan Australian Aborigines have a similar story: Koimul, a rather sullen fellow who lived in the Dreamtime, had two fire sticks and knew how to make fire, but he refused to share his secret with anyone. One day the hummingbird, Wirrit-wirrit, swooped and removed the sticks from under his arm. It was Wirrit-wirrit who shared the fire with mankind, and who to this day has two long flashing feathers in his tail.

The acquisition of wisdom and knowledge is usually associated with deities of one kind or another. In Norse mythology Odin, the foremost god in Asgard, gave an eye for a drink from the spring which would give him insight and wisdom. In Egypt Maat was the goddess of knowledge, truth and justice, while Thoth, the patron of learning, taught mortals to read and to write. In Japanese mythology Sho-Kwannon brought to all the wisdom of compassion, and Fudo Myo-o wielded a sword of knowledge against hatred and greed. In many cases the deities of wisdom were female; the Greeks, for instance, not only had Athena but also the nine Muses, who were, unlike Apollo who directed them, all female.

Wisdom was often associated with the art of healing. Both might be attributes of the same god, such as Imhotep in Egypt and Sarapis in Hellenistic Alexandria. Odin, the wise god, was also the god associated with medicine. In Greece healing was particularly the province of the god Asclepius, at whose shrines were places where mortals could be healed by a process of 'incubation' — a dreaming sleep of healing.

Many mythologies elevate the blacksmith — not always to divine status but sometimes as a helper of the gods — reflecting the importance of the craft of metalwork. In Egypt Horus had his tools manufactured by the creator god Ptah, and in eastern Siberia Boshintoi, the celestial blacksmith, was sent to teach mortals manual skills. In Indian mythology the god Twashtri forged the weapons needed; in Greece Hephaestus (Vulcan to the Romans) was the master-craftsman who made all manner of things besides weapons for his fellow Olympians, and also the famous armour of Achilles. Mjollnir, Thor's hammer, was a magical weapon of unerring accuracy — a symbol of fertility, destruction and resurrection. But Mjollnir was made by two dwarfs, Brokk and Eitri, and the concept of dwarfs producing diverse kinds of metallic objects for gods and mortals is characteristic of Norse mythology.

The Navaho Indians believed that spiders passed on the art of weaving. A mirror image of the same association is found in the Greek myth of Arachne, an obscure village girl who excelled at weaving. She challenged Athena to a contest and matched, if not surpassed her. The enraged goddess tore up the girl's work and turned her into a spider. However, Athena's anger was not simply provoked by the challenge from a mortal; she was particularly offended because *she* was the patron deity of spinning and weaving (and indeed of other crafts such as pottery and goldsmithing, overlapping with Hephaestus).

5 Quests and adventures

Stories of quests and adventures have always constituted an important part of the body of myths and legends. The quest legend is structurally similar to a picaresque novel — that is, the hero goes through a cycle of adventures and eventually reaches (or fails to reach) his goal. Many of the quest stories are long, although they can easily be divided into separate episodes or adventures. The sagas of the northern Europeans, such as *Beowulf*, are of this kind, and in Greek mythology quest legends, such as the adventures of Odysseus or Jason, abound. They are different from the 'just so' myths which explain the origin of natural phenomena; they are more developed and more complex. Quest stories usually come from more developed societies, often where the oral tradition has begun to run parallel with a written one.

The oldest known, which may date from about 3000 BC, concerns Gilgamesh, a Sumerian king of Uruk. Much of it relates his companionship and adventures with Enkidu, a wild creature originally made from clay by the goddess Aruru. But Enkidu died and Gilgamesh, devastated, set out alone to find Utnapishtim and his wife, who had been granted eternal life after building an ark and escaping a flood sent by Enlil. Gilgamesh was challenged by Utnapishtim to remain awake for a week; he failed. Utnapishtim then advised him to abandon his quest for immortality but told him where to find a plant of rejuvenation. Gilgamesh obtained the plant, only to have it stolen by a serpent. Finally, on reaching the gate of Irkalla, the underworld, Gilgamesh was able to talk with Enkidu, but his pleas for Enkidu to join him were rejected. Nergal the gatekeeper told him, 'The dead may not join the living, but the living may join the dead.' Gilgamesh fell face-down on the ground and lay there seven days, watched only by Enkidu, until he died and entered Irkalla.

One of the most famous of all quests is that of Jason, who retrieved the Golden Fleece from Colchis and returned it to Iolcos. The story recounts the adventures of a group of heroes in the ship *Argo*; the heroes were called the Argonauts and included such well-known figures as Heracles and Orpheus. Almost equally well-known are the extraordinary adventures of Odysseus, who took ten years to find his way back to his faithful wife Penelope in Ithaca. Heracles was made to perform twelve labours as a penance for killing his wife Megara and their children after Hera had afflicted him with a temporary madness. The stories of these and other tasks and exploits form a substantial quest for reconciliation with the gods (Hera remained unreconciled until Heracles died). Theseus, too, had a destiny to follow which took him to various places, including Crete, where he disposed of the half-human, half-bull Minotaur.

In other mythologies quests, searches and journeys occur too, and for a variety of reasons. Buddha's quest was for enlightenment: he set out, but the philosophers he found could not give it to him. He

became an ascetic, giving up almost everything a person could, but that was of no avail either. Finally he sat under a pipal tree and contemplated for twenty-eight days and then found what he sought. In a Persian legend contained in *Shâh-Nâme*, the hero Rustam goes through a herculean series of adventures, defeating dragons, demons and warriors while defending kings against their enemies. The knights of King Arthur's Round Table undertook a series of quests in a Christian era. (It seems likely that a historical Arthur existed in the fifth or sixth century AD, and that a considerable number of stories of different origin were attached to him later.) The major Arthurian quest was for the Holy Grail, a symbolic search for true Christendom. The Arthurian legends include Tristan and Isolde's story and are part of Celtic mythology, which ranges from the Welsh *Mabinogion* to stories from Spain, Iceland, Scandinavia, Germany and France.

When heroes went on a quest, they were often involved in fights with strange creatures. The dragons of European mythology are typical of these powerfully destructive beasts; they were strong like lions, with long serpent-like bodies, wings and fire-breathing nostrils. They were usually killed by the hero, often the symbol of good destroying evil. St George is the archetype of all dragon slayers. Modern mythological stories, such as *The Hobbit*, often include a dragon — in this case Smaug, who, like Fafnir in the northern European myths, is killed by being stabbed in his soft underbelly.

6 Battles

Famous mythological battles have occurred either near the beginning of creation to establish an order, or to change an established order, or at the end of a mythological age. A crucial battle in Greek mythology was that fought between the Titans, led by Cronos, and his children, the Olympian gods, led by Zeus. The struggle between them had continued without result for ten years — the same duration as the Trojan war. The decisive stroke was Zeus' liberation of the three Hekatonchires, creatures with a hundred hands and fifty heads. They had been imprisoned beneath the earth by Uranus (Heaven), who was father to them and the Titans. In the final battle the Titans were overwhelmed by the Hekatonchires, who could throw three hundred rocks at once. In their turn all the Titans were confined beneath the earth in the depths of Tartarus — except for Atlas, who was sent to the gate of the Garden of the Hesperides and made to hold up the sky. And so the age of the Olympian gods began.

Ragnarok is a battle to end an era — a northern European Armageddon. Although the chain of narration to which it belongs is set in the past, all reference to this annihilating climax is cast in the form of prophecy; the doom lies hidden in the future. The battle will be preceded by a three-year war in Midgard in which humans will kill each other mercilessly. That will be followed by a particularly cruel winter, Fimbulvetr, really three winters rolled into one. Then the gods and heroes will engage the giants and the forces of evil in the fiercest battle of all, Ragnarok. The morning of the battle will be marked by earthquake and flood. The heroes will stream out of Valhalla's five hundred and forty doors, eight hundred from each door — that's 432,000 in all — with Odin leading them. A universal conflagration will ensue; the Nine Worlds will become raging furnaces. Gods and heroes will die; men, women and children will die; birds and animals will die; elves and dwarves will die; the giants will all die; the monsters and the creatures of the underworld will die. But there will be a few survivors, and the land will grow green again. In the world after Ragnarok halls will be built where good gods live. The man Lif and the woman Lifthrasir, who will survive by hiding in Yggdrasil (the great ash tree linking the Nine Worlds), will have children and grandchildren, and a new order of life will begin on earth.

7 Fertility and love

Many myths and legends are associated with birth and with creation. Motherhood and fertility are associated themes. Relationships between fertility and child-bearing in humans, and fertility and fruitfulness in crops and animal husbandry are prolific. Botticelli's painting *The Birth of Venus* shows the goddess of love (Aphrodite to the Greeks) as a demure smiling figure, somewhat vulnerable as she steps ashore at Paphos on the island of Cyprus. She may appear defenceless in this Renaissance painting, but Aphrodite was one of the most powerful of the Greek goddesses. She was the goddess of love in the broadest sense, and her main purpose was to ensure conception and procreation. According to one early Greek myth she was born from the foam generated around the genitals of Uranus, which had been cut off and cast in the sea by his son Cronos. She was married to Hephaestus, but she had affairs with Ares, Adonis, Poseidon and Anchises amongst others. Eros, the god of sensual desire, was her son.

Of greater interest in the primary school are the many stories about lovers — often ill-starred, like Orpheus and Eurydice. After Orpheus had married Eurydice, a snake bit her on the ankle; she died and was taken to the underworld. Orpheus, then the world's greatest musician, was at first overcome by grief but later won his way into the underworld by singing and playing his lyre. He charmed Charon, the ferryman who took the souls of the dead across the river Styx, and passed all the dead in the underworld before reaching its ruler, Hades, and his wife Persephone. Orpheus drew on all his musical skills to win them over, and finally, after all the underworld's

inhabitants were moved to tears, Hades relented and allowed Eurydice to return with Orpheus to the world of the living. There was one condition, however: Orpheus was to lead the way and not look back at his wife. He had almost reached the outer limits of Hades' realm when he could contain himself no longer; he turned, and saw Eurydice recede into the shadows.

One of the best known stories of lovers in western tradition is that of Tristan and Isolde (sometimes the Celtic names Tristram and Iseult are used). Tristan was the nephew of King Mark of Cornwall. When he went to Ireland to seek a bride for his uncle, he slew a dragon which was ravaging the countryside and so won Isolde. On the way back from Ireland to Cornwall, Isolde inadvertently drank a magic potion which would make her fall in love with the first person she saw. She should have drunk it immediately before seeing King Mark, but the first person she saw was Tristan. The lovers' tragic story grows inevitably from the binding power of the love potion, which makes them violate the sacred bond of marriage between Isolde and King Mark.

8 Death and re-birth

Just as the early myth tellers were concerned to account for creation and the beginnings of mankind, so (like Gilgamesh) were they concerned with what happens at the end of life — with death, and also with re-birth. In the Aztec culture the god Quetzalcoatl was the god of life and the god of death.

Most mythologies have a place or places to which the souls of the departed go after death. These worlds of the dead may be as different as, say, the Viking Hel is from the Buddhist Nirvana. Many involve punishment for the misdeeds of earthly life. There are often different levels or stages, including in some cases a purgatorial stage where a refining process takes place, as in the Hindu myths about the realm of Yama. The Buddhist hell has eighteen levels of torment, some hot, some cold.

The dead often have to make a journey to 'the other side', and there are rites associated with this journey. Ships have often been used in such places as Celtic Ireland and among the ancient Egyptians and some south-east Asian peoples. Burial ships are prominent in Viking mythology.

The Greeks had stories which indicated that exceptional people could go to the underworld of Hades whilst still alive and return: Heracles, Orpheus and Odysseus all had their subterranean adventures. However, they were able to return only once; gods and goddesses alone had free passage, though they did not care to use it often. The exception was Persephone, whom Hades had abducted and taken to be his wife in the land of the dead. Angered, her mother, the corn goddess Demeter, caused a famine on earth, finally forcing Hades to agree that Persephone should spend two-thirds of each year with her and only one-third with him.

As noted earlier, Persephone's return to the upper world every year is essentially a fertility myth. It was central to the cult of Demeter at her shrine in Eleusis, near Athens, and it is likely that the famous Eleusinian Mysteries came to associate the regeneration of crops with ideas of human immortality. Details remain obscure, however; the secrets of the ritual were never made public. But ideas of rebirth and reincarnation occur in other mythologies: for instance, the Egyptian phoenix was a symbol of rejuvenation and the return of the sun. It was believed that when it grew old, the phoenix would set fire to its nest and and emerge from the flames reborn.

An unusual, almost bizarre version of the ever-living is Saehrimnir, a boar slaughtered each day by the cook in Valhalla and boiled in a cauldron to feed the host of warriors. No matter how much they stuffed themselves, the meat of the boar was always sufficient — and the beast returned to life in time to be slaughtered again the next morning.

Immortality is a characteristic of gods and goddesses. Perhaps the Greek gods still live on Mt Olympus — at least the myths do not destroy them. Perhaps the gods of the Aztecs and the Incas survived the assaults of the Conquistadors. One thing is certain, however: for countless contemporary believers, divinities live on and the truths embodied in their myths live on.

~CHAPTER THREE~

THE CLASSROOM AUDIENCE

As we have seen, most myths and legends are stories which were originally passed on by word of mouth. The classroom is one of the best places to continue that tradition. The teacher should become the storyteller — the bard, poet or minstrel. Of course children are always telling each other stories and jokes and recalling their experiences; it's a natural part of growing up. But equally they love being told stories, and myths and legends offer many marvellous stories to tell.

Storytelling and story reading

Storytelling derives from the oral tradition, whereas story reading depends on the tradition of the written text. There's nothing right or wrong about either of these approaches; primary children need their teachers to use both. It's rather a question of what is appropriate — and, given the origin of most myths and legends in the oral tradition, I believe that it may well be preferable to treat them in a storytelling way rather than always relying on a written text and reading them aloud.

While storytelling and story reading are both social experiences, storytelling is more akin to the way that people usually talk to each other. This gives the storyteller certain advantages. A spoken text can be varied extensively as a story is being told. Just think of telling a joke — you have the gist and the punch line in your head, but then you improvise to suit the occasion and your audience. Likewise the storyteller can speed up by compressing or omitting sections, or slow down by expanding and filling in details — options not so readily available to the story reader, who is much more closely bound to the printed text. The storyteller can invent details calculated to appeal to that particular audience, and can generally react to the audience more freely than the story reader. To a certain extent the reader's text gets in the way, for the act of reading necessarily restricts eye contact between the reader and the audience. But the storyteller has no intervening text and so can enjoy almost constant eye contact. A good storyteller watches the audience intensely and accommodates them by varying the story according to the feedback received.

In addition, the storyteller can use body language to a far greater extent than the story reader: gestures and facial expressions — even movement — can enhance a storytelling. The teacher as teller can enter the world of myths and legends and bring them alive for the listening children. In story reading, however, it is largely the personality of the author which the children perceive, because it is almost always the author's text they are hearing, not the teacher's.

Nevertheless teachers may sometimes find the literary quality of a written version so impressive that a rehearsed reading of the text promises to have more impact on the class than their own retelling. This is particularly likely to happen with versions by such respected authors as Kevin Crossley-Holland, Rosemary Sutcliff, Roger Lancelyn Green or Ian Serraillier, which are a world apart from the simple narrative outline that may be found in a reference book. In such cases the power, drama or beauty of the author's words and images will probably compensate for some loss of immediate contact with the audience. Indeed, as Elizabeth Cook has so ably demonstrated in *The Ordinary and the Fabulous*, the comparison of different written versions of the same story can be a rewarding study in itself.

A good classroom literature program provides plenty of opportunity for children to read for themselves and talk with others about what they have read. Therefore, in addition to telling myths and legends and sometimes reading them aloud, teachers should encourage children to read them independently. Picture book versions of individual stories are ideal to start with, and once older children are familiar with a number of stories within a particular tradition (for example, creation myths from various cultures, or Norse mythology), they will be better able to read for themselves the longer versions which are available separately or, more often, in collections. Some ideas for developing a 'genre study' around myths and legends are suggested in the next chapter.

Continuing the oral tradition

Teachers who tell stories in the classroom will find that storytelling is best seen as a friendly, informal occasion, with both teacher and children relaxed. Most classrooms seem to have four corners, with the door usually occupying one. A balanced language classroom has a second for reading and a third for writing, while the fourth is the story corner. The story corner (or even a mat) provides a congenial setting, away from the formality of desks and chairs arranged in rows or groups, and such a setting is essential to successful storytelling, even for children at the top end of the primary school. It helps to establish an atmosphere of enjoyment in which teller and listeners can concentrate on the story.

Storytelling occasions should be uninterrupted, and so teachers should select a time when they know they are unlikely to be disturbed by the crackle of the public address system or by someone coming in to settle a bundle of administrative queries. The importance and distinctive atmosphere of a storytelling session can also be enhanced by devices such as a chair or stool on which the teacher always sits to tell or read a story, or a special storytelling coat with large pockets to hold objects or books related to the story.

Telling a story, such as a myth or legend, means that the teacher has a little learning to do. This is really much easier than many teachers think, and it certainly doesn't require the long working out of stories in the excellent manner of the Australian storytellers guilds. Members of a storytellers guild usually spend many hours preparing, rehearsing and practising in front of an audience composed of fellow members before they tell a story publicly. They work towards a polished performance, and their willingly given services can certainly be used on special occasions in schools. However, for teachers in the classroom, I tend to play down the performance aspect and discourage activities which require an inordinate amount of preparation. I believe that storytelling should be a normal part of the language curriculum, rather than a once-a-year or once-a-term special occasion.

The minstrel bard who regaled a hall full of Greeks or Vikings with his version of a myth or legend would usually start with an outline, a bare skeletal structure. The art of storytelling lay in the 'fleshing out' of the skeleton. Two important considerations which helped shape the minstrel's art were, first, the purpose of telling the story and, second, the audience. They were of course closely linked. A major purpose of telling myths and legends (besides providing entertainment) would be to strengthen the group identity and cohesion of the audience. The minstrel would want to encourage his listeners, make them feel important and reinforce links to their heritage. Equally he would want to fill out his story in terms which they understood: he would use a language they were familiar with (although it would not necessarily be identical with the language they used every day) and he would refer to things they knew. In other words, the skeleton was always fleshed out in a way which made the story intelligible to the listener and enjoyable.

This is just what you need to do in the classroom — and to help do it, I'd suggest writing a simple outline consisting of the headings of main events. For example, on one occasion when I told stories about Heracles to a Year 6 class, there were some 'labours' I felt unsure about as it had been a long time since I'd read them. One was the capture of the Apples of the Hesperides (the eleventh labour), and to ensure that I remembered the events in sequence, I used the skeleton shown in the diagram overleaf.

Learning a skeleton is no substitute for knowing the story, but it is the starting point. If you read a story in one of the versions given in the lists at the back of this book, make your skeleton as you go through the story for the second time. (Incidentally, you might prefer to make a slightly more complicated form of skeleton, as suggested by Baker and Greene [1977].) Then, using the skeleton as a prompt, try telling the story to yourself in front of the bathroom mirror — or anywhere else you can be secure in your solitude. You'll probably find that the skeleton is easier to memorise than you

> **XI The Apples of the Hesperides**
> - *H. visits Nereus first*
> - *Kills the dragon Ladon*
> - *Atlas gets the apples*
> - *H. tricks Atlas, sets off with the apples*
> - *Antaios in Libya*
> - *Busiris in Egypt*
> - *H. goes to Caucusus Mountains to release Prometheus*
> - *Gives apples to Eurystheus, who returns them*
> - *Gives apples to Athena, who returns them to the Garden of the Hesperides*

expect. It will also help if you try to visualise the action as if it were a play, film or television drama. If your source includes illustrations, they will help you to see it happening. Retelling the story will require you to adopt Coleridge's 'willing suspension of disbelief' and tell it as if you saw it all happen only yesterday.

A bridge from reading to telling

Let me suggest one approach for teachers who would like to find an easy way into storytelling which begins at only a small remove from story reading.

A1 Select a short myth such as 'Baldur's Dreams' and read it several times. (A possible source would be *The Norse Myths* by Kevin Crossley-Holland, pp. 168–70.)

A2 Prepare some background material (especially if this is the first Norse myth you have retold), including large charts and wall illustrations. For example, write on a chart the different names Odin is called in the story. Use single words and short phrases only. Pin the charts in a convenient visible place in the classroom. They are there for the children of course, but they will also help you tell the story.

A3 Make a copy of the text and mark changes which you think will help you reach the children to whom you will be 'reading' the story. Make the language more informal; move it closer to the way you usually talk.

A4 'Read' the story to the children, making the changes as you go. Sometimes you may read a few sentences word for word, but mostly you will adapt; summarise or extend as appropriate.

B A second myth (perhaps related) can be treated similarly until stage 3, when you leave the printed text unmarked except for putting asterisks in the margin against the important parts of the story. Then, instead of reading any of the text, you tell the story in your own words, keeping the asterisked pages before you merely as a prompt.

C By the time you get to your third myth you will be ready to make the sort of skeleton I have already described. You should also use any pictures that occur in your source(s) to supplement the skeleton.

It's worth mentioning here two books simultaneously published in 1991 under the same title (*Children as Storytellers*), as both have useful sections on ways to learn a story. Kerry Mallan's book gives a further development of what I have called a 'skeleton' in the section dealing with structures and maps (pp. 33–51), while Claire Jennings' book has a rather shorter section which deals with visual imagery, webs and maps (pp. 32–41).

Adapting content and language

Fitting the story to your audience (as the poets and myth tellers have done for centuries) requires special attention to two matters. Firstly, you need to screen the content carefully. Many myths and legends from around the world contain sexual and violent elements. The threshold of acceptability is a matter for individual judgement, and much will depend on what you know of your class, as well as on general school policy. However, although there are no hard and fast rules, most of us would agree that the story of how Pasiphaë mated with the Cretan bull to produce the Minotaur is not an obvious choice for young children. Yet while stories like this may seem to exclude themselves, others may be judged acceptable as long as the more robust elements of the tradition are modified or left out. For example, when telling the story of Heracles' death, I usually start with his marriage to Deianara and include the episode where the centaur Nessus assaults her (it's an attempted rape). Nessus, dying from an arrow shot by Heracles, tells Deianara to collect the blood from his wound and the semen he has spilt on the ground and to save the mixture as it will have the power to keep Heracles faithful. I find it easy to skirt round the rape nature of the assault, and the story works perfectly well without any mention of the semen.

The second matter is the language of the story. In fleshing out the skeleton version of the selected myth or legend, you will easily be able to adapt your language to whatever level will suit the children who are to listen. In one sense, of course, there is nothing to adapt (as there is when a printed story is read) and for the most part you will talk to the children as you normally would. For instance, when Heracles returns to the cowardly King Eurystheus at the end of each labour, I make him say, 'Been there! Done that!' To use contemporary colloquialisms is not merely in order but should be encouraged — it helps bring the story alive.

However, it would be a mistake to assume that the language of storytelling is exactly the same as everyday spoken language. In order to hold and entertain an audience, the storyteller manipulates language — perhaps using a series of short sentences to create a sense of urgency as the narrative moves towards its climax, perhaps dwelling occasionally on the description of some character or object to create a stronger visual image. Nor should storytelling teachers necessarily restrict themselves to language that's well within their audience's current understanding. Storytelling provides opportunities for introducing children to unfamiliar syntactic constructions and for extending their vocabulary. The written versions of myths and legends listed at the back of this book contain, in contexts which make their meaning clear, many somewhat unusual words selected to excite a sense of wonder or drama: for example, 'perished', 'perils', 'loathsome' or 'flounder'. A teacher who knows his or her class and is sensitive to children's responses in the storytelling session will be able to judge just what is appropriate.

Sometimes storytelling conventions will be prominent. Even the youngest listeners know that 'Once upon a time' signals many things: that *this* is a story, that it is probably set in the distant past, that there will be characters who do things and to whom things happen. There are various conventional phrases which act as markers in a story, signalling to listeners what is significant or helping them make connections between ideas. As you read myths and legends yourself, you will begin to recognise some of them and build them into your storytelling — for example, 'And so it was that . . . ', 'With these words . . . ', 'Behold . . . '. The teacher's storytelling language can become a very effective bridge between children's everyday oral language and the more formal literary language of books.

Memory aids

There may be times when the mind goes blank and the storyteller is at a loss for words, and you will need some kind of insurance against this. There are several kinds of memory aids which may help, and three I have found useful are suggested below. First, however, I should say that I'd expect you always to have a source book containing the myth or legend close at hand to refer to if needed. This is not an admission of defeat but a sensible precaution, and in any case the book may well be needed for reasons other than as a prompt.

My first memory aid is, as you might expect, a skeleton like the one already discussed and illustrated. It can be kept in the hand or in any position where a quick glance enables you to read it. Although the 'Apples of the Hesperides' skeleton is probably intelligible only to me, since I wrote it, you will use your own prompt words and phrases when you write one, and that is all that will be needed. Children much prefer you to glance at the skeleton rather than mumble and wander on your way through the story. And a second's glance, even a second glance, will not impede the narrative flow.

Another memory aid you can use is a set of flash cards showing unusual or difficult names of people and places, or significant objects which form part of the story. I write these on large cards, like the one shown overleaf for Deianara, and then stack them in the order in which they enter the story. I introduce each one to the audience as the story proceeds, placing them where the children can see them. I can then refer to them during the storytelling, and this is especially

> Deianara

helpful when the story is part of a series and one character appears in several episodes. It's also useful to have the cards available for the children to refer to in any activity which follows the storytelling. Many of the names are difficult to remember and even harder to spell, and so these cards become reference material.

I may also make use of illustrations in my source book as a memory aid — though what I can do with them obviously depends on what's there. However, most of the texts written for children will include some illustrations, even if there tend to be fewer in books aimed at older children. Admittedly this third memory aid is less useful than the first two, but very often a section of the story goes along well when there are details to dwell on in a picture. For example, Ian Serraillier's *Heracles the Strong* has a simple line drawing showing Eurystheus hiding from Heracles in a large bronze pot. I found this to be a very effective illustration when going through a cycle of stories about Heracles, and it was a feature of the semester's stories which the children remembered vividly.

The visual dimension

Most teachers will have their own preferences about the kinds of book illustrations which are most useful in the classroom (though they will have to accommodate to the fact that many of the books containing myths and legends have been around for long enough for the illustrations as well as the language to seem a little dated now). My own preference is for simplicity and so I incline towards line drawings, which tend to concentrate on the essential details. It is true that some archaeological illustrations (i.e. photographs of artefacts) are very clear and illuminating, but others are less helpful and may contain specialised detail which has taken experts years to understand. None the less, if any illustration promises to have some meaning for your audience, do share it with them — after all, why would you want to deny them something you've seen and used in realising the meaning of the story yourself?

It's also worth remarking that when illustrated versions of myths and legends are included, even temporarily, in the classroom library, children are able to explore the illustrations at their leisure and extend the mental images they have formed while listening to or reading a story. Some illustrated books are particularly evocative and deserve closer scrutiny. For example, the melting of Icarus' wax-bound wings after he has disobeyed his father and flown too close to the sun is brilliantly evoked in the illustrations that accompany the text of Penelope Farmer's *Daedalus and Icarus*.

Older children will enjoy poring over the illustrations by Giovanni Caselli for Brian Branston's *Gods and Heroes from Viking Mythology*, or those by Robert Ingpen for Maurice Saxby's *The Great Deeds of Superheroes* and *The Great Deeds of Heroic Women*. And no sharing of Aboriginal lore would be complete without the opportunity for children to explore the illustrations of Raymond Meeks or Dick Roughsey.

Of course book illustrations are not your only resource. The story corner of the classroom should evoke the setting of the myths and legends to be told. Say you have chosen some from Greek mythology, such as those about Odysseus — then display maps of Greece and the Mediterranean world. Visit tourist agencies for posters of Greece's classical heritage. Enlarge illustrations from your source books on the photocopier. Cover the walls of the corner to make a visual context for the stories — and don't forget to refer to the maps and pictures on display during your retellings. That way the children will not only enjoy a richer background at the time they first hear the stories, but will also have more to draw on in any follow-up work they do later.

Finally, as a storyteller, you can sometimes make effective use of dramatic 'props'. It does not take a great deal of effort, for example, to recreate with cardboard and silver foil Perseus' winged sandals, the sharp sickle so important to his quest, or the mirrored shield loaned to him by Athena. A spray of gold paint can turn ordinary apples into the golden apples of the Hesperides. And on another occasion you might unravel a ball of thread as you tell how Ariadne helped Theseus to find his way through the labyrinth of King Minos.

~ CHAPTER FOUR ~

WHAT NEXT?

Many authors have filled books with advice about what to do in teaching literature, ranging from recommendations for short activities to the more substantial (and excellent) writing of the contributors to *Give Them Wings* (Saxby & Winch 1987). While I don't propose to provide a précis of such ideas, it is important to recognise that much of what has been said about literature in the classroom generally applies to the published texts of myths and legends which form part of the wide array of children's literature. What is different is the oral nature of their origins, and the suggestions which follow assume a literary diet high in the richness of storytelling.

1 Do nothing! Yes, do nothing

It is important that children get time for reflection, time to savour the experience of the storytelling or reading, and time to retain the enjoyment. It is a fallacy to assume that there must always be a follow-up activity, that every text presented to children must somehow be 'substantiated' for language development to take place. I have found that some myths and legends can have such a powerful emotional impact that it would be verging on sacrilege to disturb it by going over the story again. As teachers we must not forget

Wordsworth's claim — 'We murder to dissect'. Time your telling of a myth or legend to end at a natural break in the school day, and don't presume that children will forget a story if it's not reinforced.

2 Let children become tellers of myths and legends

Children now become part of the storytelling chain (here the books by Kerry Mallan and Claire Jennings mentioned in the previous chapter are your best starting points). This isn't really a question of introducing children to something new because, as I've previously remarked, they are already telling each other about their own experiences and regaling each other with anecdotes, jokes, riddles and retellings of some of the narrative-structured TV programs, films and videos they have watched. However, like the bard and the minstrel, children can become aware of broader purposes and audiences for their retellings. It is good to encourage them to retell to friends, peers and siblings myths and legends they have heard or read. I also feel that they can tell their teacher, parent or another adult about a myth or legend they have been asked to research. (An oral presentation of their 'project' is of course entirely appropriate to the oral origin of most myths and legends.) Perhaps a sympathetic adult ear can be used for a practice run before a story is retold to a group or class. Usually the child whose purpose for retelling a myth or legend is to share real enjoyment of the story will be a successful storyteller.

More than other types of literature, myths and legends deal with the fantastic and supernatural, as well as the clever and brave. This is part of their appeal for children, whose interest in what normal humans cannot achieve is sometimes all-consuming. Such interest in the abnormal can easily extend to horror visions of Grendel leaving a trail of blood across the marshes after Beowulf has wrenched his arm off, or to baleful anticipation of the consequences of Tristan and Isolde drinking the love potion before they reach King Mark in Cornwall. It is because so much of the substance of myths and legends lies beyond the plane of ordinary reality — like a man whose grip has the strength of thirty men or a drink that will make the drinkers fall hopelessly in love with each other — that the stories appeal to children. They readily retell them to each other because they aren't ordinary.

3 Let children write

Retelling
Given that any telling of a myth or legend is a *retelling*, encourage children to write their own versions of ones they have heard or read, and then to illustrate and publish their writing. Children who find it difficult to come up with original story ideas will find that in myths and legends they have a rich source of material to stimulate narrative writing. Equally those experiencing difficulty in developing their narratives and providing a satisfactory resolution will find relatively simple narrative structures upon which to experiment, as well as successful models of episodic structures with a series of complications (in the style of much film and television material).

Children can be encouraged to publish their retellings for audiences beyond the class. One obvious audience is another, possibly younger class in the school. Pairs or small groups of children can be responsible for producing their own 'big book' versions of favourite myths or legends. If a number of pairs or groups chose to retell the same story, there will later be opportunities to compare and contrast the different versions. The activity may well benefit from some teacher scaffolding, aimed at helping children to:
- select the elements essential to their retelling
- choose which events to illustrate and the style of illustration
- decide how to divide their final text into separate pages to accommodate the illustrations.

If separate writing and illustrating teams are formed, it may help to focus on different ideas for illustrations and make children more aware of the close relationship between pictures and text.

Exploring story structure
While most children will choose to retell the events of a story in chronological order, you can deliberately use a myth or legend with which children are familiar to help them understand how authors can manipulate narrative elements to achieve particular effects. For example, older primary children retelling the story of the death of Baldur can start at the point where Hod is about to fire the mistletoe arrow, then explain how such a situation arose and finish with the death of Baldur and the attempts to free him from Hel. I have found

that older primary children do sometimes like to start at an interesting point in a story which is not the chronological beginning. There is of course a long-established precedent for this in Homer's *Odyssey*, a model followed by Virgil in the *Aeneid* and Milton in *Paradise Lost*.

Looking at 'literary' language

If children who have made themselves familiar with the same published version of a myth or legend individually compose their own written retellings, they can then join in pairs to compare their versions. They should look for similarities and differences not only in what they have chosen to include or omit but also in the wording of their retellings. Finally they can compare their retellings with a copy of the original text. By this time their comparisons should have made them more sensitive to the choices of vocabulary and phrasing made by the author. In a group or class sharing, children can suggest particular examples of 'literary' language they have noticed in the original and the equivalents they have used in their own retellings.

Innovating

Besides retelling myths and legends, children can be encouraged to create new stories involving the same characters. Once they have understood the broad situation and typical pattern of events as well as the characters involved, it becomes relatively easy to create some apocryphal adventures. For example, a Year 6 group with whom I recently shared a series of stories about Heracles suggested a thirteenth labour for him to accomplish, as Eurystheus was not satisfied with the twelfth. The group recognised Heracles' predilection for wrestling, his favourite weapons (such as his club and bow) and his experience in ridding society of destructive beasts and inhuman humans. With these patterns established, they were able to suggest plots for a further adventure, which some of them wrote about.

One note of caution should be sounded here. Sometimes, after sharing with their classes traditional Aboriginal lore, teachers ask children to write their own creation stories. While this may appear an innocuous practice, teachers should be mindful of the spiritual importance of such lore to the Aboriginal community. The writing of 'new' Dreamtime stories could be seen in the same light as the writing of 'new' parables after a reading of the New Testament.

Some children are interested in filling gaps, in writing about what could have happened but is not recorded. The challenge then is to create plausible details and at the same time maintain narrative interest. Two eleven-year-old girls, Jasmine and Elizabeth, based their work on the hostility between Zeus and his consort Hera after Zeus had seduced a mortal, Alcmena, who became the mother of Heracles. This is what they thought might have happened on Mount Olympus:

WHO WILL BE KING?

The King of Athens has just passed away and Hera and Zeus are arguing about who should be the next King of Athens.

ZEUS: Hera, I think the best king for Athens is Heracles.
HERA: Well I think it should be Eurystheus. Just think: 'King Eurystheus'. Doesn't it sound brave and bold?
ZEUS: A bold name would never suit such a coward. Heracles deserves to be king after all his good deeds for people.
HERA: He has many muscles but a pea-sized brain!
ZEUS: If he had such a small brain, how did he come up with the idea for cleaning the stables of Augeas?
HERA: Look at Eurystheus! He has experienced being a great leader. Heracles has not!
ZEUS: Why should he have two chances if Heracles has had none?
HERA: But Heracles has no brain to match his muscles. All he would do is make mistakes.
ZEUS: That is not the way he would rule a city. Heracles can be smart if he wishes to be. You must not underestimate him. Hera, he is no ordinary mortal.
HERA: Why don't you even consider my choice? If you think about my choice for once, you'll like it!
ZEUS: The choice is Heracles and that is that!
HERA: OK, but if Heracles dies, my Eurystheus is king.
ZEUS: No! It'll always be my choice. Eurystheus will never be king as long as I am King of the Gods!
HERA: Then you should not be King of the Gods as long as you cannot make the right decision!

After fighting throughout the night, they decided that Zetar would be a good king, but they still thought their own decisions were the best but they didn't say anything.

Writing playscripts

The dialogue imagined by Jasmine and Elizabeth is more than halfway to a playscript, and this is another form of writing that many myths and legends lend themselves to. It's also one which can be rewardingly explored by partnerships. Of course children need to be familiar not only with the story they are adapting to dramatic form but also with the conventions and layout of a playscript, and so you may need to help them find some appropriate published models and support their efforts in other ways. Through discussion with you, they will come to realise that the narrative elements of the story will either have to be adapted to dialogue or action (with stage directions), or else attributed to one or more 'narrators'. You can show them how to use variously coloured highlighter pens to mark the extant dialogue on a photocopy of the story, which can later be cut up and pasted into the script. If the playscript is to be 'published' for later reading, or for rehearsal and performance, the draft script should be tried out in front of a group of children from the class. This group could be asked to check that the play makes sense — i.e. that all the necessary characters, action, dialogue and changes of scene are included, and that the play flows logically without reference back to the original story.

Language experience

Many teachers in the junior primary grades use 'language experience' (Sloan & Latham 1981) as an element in their reading-writing program. Usually this involves a 'hands-on' experience as the beginning and basis for subsequent written language work, but it can also work well if you substitute a myth or legend (either told or read to the class) as the focal point. You should make generous use of illustrations and relevant artefacts (such as a stuffed toy snake for the Australian Aboriginal story of the Rainbow Serpent), and also exploit gestures and other body language in your storytelling or reading. Casting anchor, shooting an arrow and other such movements can then be repeated by the children as they 'rehearse' parts of the story.

In normal versions of language experience the teacher may write on the board words and phrases children use in their retellings of the experience; in this variation you can write children's responses to questions about the story, such as 'What did you like best? or 'How did Jason travel to find the Golden Fleece?' After writing the children's text, you can both read it to them and get them to read it, as well as using the text to confirm their understanding of the language features involved.

Journal writing
A variant of the retellings already suggested is journal or log writing. Because many myths and legends involve journeys or quests, they can legitimately be used as a stimulus for this kind of writing, providing that children have already been made familiar with its features. Taking on the persona of the main character (which requires trying to see events from that character's point of view), upper primary children can write in the first person the daily journal of, say, Perseus, Heracles or Jason. Alternatively, a more 'objective' record of the sequence of events could be kept in the ship's log of the *Argo*.

4 Keeping track of a story

Even when myths and legends are simply told, their plots may be quite involved and complex. In the 'hero tales' of Greek or Norse mythology, for instance, there are commonly numerous changes of setting, with new characters and events for listeners or readers to keep track of in each new location. There is also the difficulty of remembering the particular attributes of gods and mortals. Constructing a story map is one way in which less experienced readers can keep track of a story's sequence of events, settings and characters. However, even if children are familiar with the technique from previous literature-based classroom work, I'd suggest that you first demonstrate it by jointly constructing a story map with the class, perhaps using an appropriate myth or legend with which children are already familiar.

It may also be helpful for children to draw up charts like the one shown opposite. As they reread (or recall) the story, they work individually or in pairs, listing in the charts important story information that needs to be incorporated in their maps. Next they

examine the charts and explore ways of representing visually the written summaries they contain. For example, in the story of Demeter and Persephone, the beginning of which is charted here, children would need to consider and perhaps discuss in small groups how they could also represent:
- the wide-ranging search by Demeter's servants
- Demeter's journey across the sea
- the failure of crops in her absence
- her disguise at Eleusis, and so on.

After sharing their ideas, children can work individually or in pairs to construct their maps, later exchanging them and making comparisons.

SETTING	MAJOR CHARACTERS	EVENTS
the mountainous island of Sicily	Demeter (goddess of the harvest) Persephone (her beloved daughter)	Mother and daughter lived happily together. Crops grew plentifully.
a hillside	Persephone Hades (god of the underworld)	P. was gathering flowers. H. snatched her up in his chariot drawn by two black horses and carried her off beneath the earth.

5 Literary lifeboat

This activity postulates that a lifeboat crammed with story characters is sinking and one has to be heaved overboard. It can be a useful way of exploring the function of different characters in a myth or legend. Children work in groups, and each child or group has to argue why the character they represent is essential to the story and cannot be thrown out. As this activity is based on discussion, it is especially valuable in developing the use of rhetoric (language intended to persuade).

6 Interpreting myths and legends through drama

Myths and legends are full of the elements upon which drama turns: confrontations between characters (Beowulf and Grendel); dilemmas for which a solution must be worked out (escape from a monster such as the Cyclops or the Minotaur); brave and heroic actions, or still moments of great poignancy (Orpheus and Eurydice). Turning myths and legends into drama can be a most rewarding activity for children, and some suggestions for writing playscripts have already been given. The success of a dramatised version will depend on several factors, including the appropriateness of the story; however, I feel that the most significant factor will be the teacher's own enthusiasm for the story and the way in which it is retold or read to the children.

Improvisation

Although re-enacting a story may lead to somewhat mechanical repetition, it is often useful to start with this, especially with younger children. Use part if not all of a myth or legend, allowing the story to stay close to the original but with the children incorporating their own details. Younger children can begin by miming actions while you (or a child) tell the story. The children feel safe because the 'drama' is not relying on memory but arises from cues given by the narration. It is then quite easy to move on to adding words to the actions, or to developing movement which expresses feelings rather than simply imitating actions.

As children get older, themes from myths and legends can be worked out in a different context or setting. One example for upper primary school children, based on the story of Pandora's box, can be found in the Tasmanian publication *A Framework for Speech and Drama* (Drama Booklet, p. 45). Another example might be based on the apples of Idun, which were believed to keep the Norse gods young — stories about contemporary equivalents to keep humans eternally young can be created in dramatic form by middle primary pupils.

Divide the class into small groups and provide them with discussion questions which will help them to take up the idea of the desirability of an elixir of life and devise a story around it. What food do we now eat which might become an apple of eternal youth? How does it become known? What happens when the discovery occurs? What might be the disadvantage (e.g. everything stays young except the voice)? What is the result of this one drawback? How is the story resolved? After discussion, the improvised dramas can be tried out and then presented by the different groups.

The teacher in role
There are times when you will remain outside the drama and speak to the children as their teacher. On other occasions you will need to adopt a role within the drama, usually a controlling or linking one which will enable you to give its events some cohesion. This is particularly the case with younger children or with dramas involving the whole class, when your support will be invaluable in maintaining the storyline and ensuring that improvisation does not degenerate into the stereotyped actions characteristic of TV cartoon heroes.

Readers theatre
Many teachers find readers theatre techniques an attractive way into drama, since the 'actors' rely not on learning a script but on reading one, and can do without props and costumes. Moreover, to present a story successfully to the rest of the class, the performing group needs to be not only thoroughly familiar with the story but also confident of their interpretation — something which they should arrive at through discussion with each other and perhaps with you. Readers theatre can thus be a valuable strategy for developing comprehension skills.

If children are to prepare their own performing scripts (which is highly desirable), they will need to learn the necessary skills through the sort of modelling and scaffolding exemplified by one teacher of a class of seven- and eight-year-olds. She had been sharing with them the series of simple retellings of Aboriginal lore compiled by Pamela Lofts with the help of bilingual Aboriginal children. To introduce readers theatre, she began by writing her own script for *Warnayarra: The Rainbow Snake*. She distributed copies to a group of children, explained how it was derived from the story and let them compare it with the original text. Next she helped them to rehearse a performance, which was duly given before the rest of the class with great success.

The group then decided they would like to adapt another of the stories themselves and settled on *How the Kangaroos Got Their Tails*. The teacher worked with them over the first session, helping them make decisions about who the characters were and whether it was necessary to include a storyteller (it was). The group, now working independently, marked dialogue on a photocopy of the story with different coloured marker pens. The teacher's help was needed again in putting together the script (a mixture of 'cut and paste' and the children's writing) and in rehearsing the presentation. This was also well received by the class, and the teacher now felt confident enough to allow this small group to continue with less support while she introduced the strategy to another group.

There are a number of publications now available for teachers interested in trying readers theatre. In PEN 79 *True Wizardry* by Marion Robertson, teachers will find an excellent introduction to the technique which will give them a flying start. Incidentally, there are usually no copyright problems in using myths and legends for readers theatre.

Radio plays
With their possibilities for dramatic dialogue and sound effects, myths and legends often convert well to rehearsal and recording as 'radio plays', and the kind of adaptation required is quite like that involved in producing a readers theatre script. Completed scripts can be recorded and broadcast over the school public address system during a rainy lunchtime, or kept in the library or near the classroom listening post for individual and small group listening. Like readers theatre, this activity focuses attention on the listener and can be particularly useful in helping children to keep an audience in mind for both their written and oral communication.

Dance drama
The action, grandeur and distant perspectives of myths and legends make them good material for improvisation through dance, and small groups of children, particularly those with an interest in dance, may wish to develop their improvisations to a performance standard. Your help will probably be needed as children select stories suitable for interpretation through movement — look for ones with plenty of

dramatic action but not too complex a sequence of events. You can also provide a bank of tapes of suggestive music. Don't limit yourself to contemporary pop: try some Sibelius or Grieg for a Norse story, or tracks from some of the Stravinsky ballets, such as *The Firebird, The Rite of Spring, Apollo* or *The Fairy's Kiss* (which is based on Tchaikovsky themes). If you keep in the classroom a 'prop box' of odds and ends, you can suggest simple ideas that children can readily take up to dramatic effect: a long piece of soft blue fabric can easily become a swirling ocean (Beowulf or Odysseus); streamers of yellow crepe paper can transform children into the burning rays of the sun (Daedalus and Icarus).

7 Interpretation through art and craft

Right from the beginning of school, children love to draw pictures to accompany the stories they write, and they should certainly be encouraged to illustrate any myths and legends they write about or retell. Myths and legends are also an ideal means of linking literature to the classroom program for visual arts. Listeners and readers often create strong mental images of settings, characters or events, and these can be realised both as a valid artistic experience and as a means of revealing their understanding of a story.

Myths and legends lend themselves to a wide range of artistic interpretation, from illustrating stories in drawing and painting to recreating some of the characteristic artefacts and buildings. I have seen a variety of Mjollnir hammers, each the product of different children who gave me their own versions of how Thor used Mjollnir. The eight-legged horse Sleipnir from the same set of Viking myths has been painted by children who had various ideas about the position of the legs — some thought they were evenly distributed along the sides, others that there were four at the front and four at the rear. Some legendary beasts and monsters lend themselves to mask-making. The masks can become part of a classroom display, or they can be designed for use in drama or dance-drama activities — a bull's head can easily turn an eleven year old boy into a minotaur!

Illustrating a sequence of events
As a complement to a written retelling, children can retell the story in a series of labelled pictures, perhaps for wall display. Older children

may prefer to draw the story in comic-book style. Children can also be challenged to work in small groups to produce a wall frieze of a chosen story. The groups should first discuss the way they will approach the task, including what significant events to include and possible media and style. Next individuals or pairs from each group could take responsibility for creating one panel. Finally the groups would reconvene to assemble the frieze and perhaps create a text to accompany it.

Creating a collage
Another challenging way for children to interpret stories they have read or heard is to create a collage in paint and 'found' objects. More abstract and symbolic than a frieze, the collage should capture both the mood of the story and its most significant images. If the collage is a group enterprise, children should first recall (or reread) the story, brainstorming and listing the images they believe are most significant and how they might best be portrayed. For example, for the story of Demeter and Persephone mentioned earlier in this chapter, children might choose as significant images seeds bursting into shoot and shimmering cornfields, and, by contrast, wasted crops and the shadows of the underworld. The discussion a group of children engage in when planning a collage requires them to think very carefully about the story's events and what they make of them.

8   Linking myths and legends with other curriculum areas

Myths and legends are usually associated with people-based studies such as anthropology, religion and other social sciences. In primary schools the traditional stories of particular peoples can be included in the social studies aspects of the curriculum. The most obvious opportunity in Australia is the sharing of Aboriginal lore as part of the class Aboriginal studies program. The life and culture of Aboriginal Australians have been so closely intertwined with stories of the Dreamtime that any study of them is really impossible without considering Aboriginal lore. In this classroom context the stories are presented as part of the belief systems of the Aboriginal people, rather than being told simply for their story value. The same would apply to the myths and legends of other surviving cultural groups, such as American Indians. Of course the Dreamtime is not a thing of the past to many contemporary Aboriginal people, and so there is all the more reason to find out as much as you can from local Aboriginal groups or some of the excellent reference materials now available before sharing Aboriginal lore with your class.

Myths and legends can also link up with other areas of the curriculum, such as measurement work in mathematics. For example, while I was enjoying the story of Beowulf with a class of middle primary children, we recreated Beowulf's boat. Using statistics from a Viking ship found at Gokstad in Norway, the children measured the outline of the boat on the school yard (it was 23.33 metres long and 5.25 metres wide). The shape was judged from photographs of the excavated Norwegian ship and marked out with blocks of wood. Small chairs were then placed in position for the Viking oarsmen. All this helped to give some realism to the setting for Beowulf's story.

9 Reading-based activities

There are a number of ways in which the study of myths and legends can be linked to a literature-based reading program, especially with upper primary classes. Such a program assumes a good stock of books for children to choose from and library support is important, for in most cases the relevant books will be housed in libraries outside the classroom — especially the colourful but expensive collections in large volumes. So, before embarking on one of the options suggested below, you will need time to assemble a temporary bulk loan of between thirty and forty different books from the school and local libraries. If there aren't enough available, you may need to make photocopies, checking first that you are complying with copyright law.

Library services are also needed when teachers and children want to research the background to myths and legends. Given sufficient warning, librarians are always willing to obtain the resources needed to support any topic or theme which a teacher wishes to emphasise, and myths and legends are no exception.

A genre study
A literary genre study involves the teacher and class (or even one small group from the class) in investigating the features of a particular genre through reading lots of examples and making comparisons. If

there are sufficient books available, it's best at the start to limit your scope. For instance, you might examine only creation myths, or Arthurian legends, or stories of the Greek or Norse heroes. Your overarching question is 'What things can we say that all these stories have in common?' This will probably need to be broken down into more specific questions, viz:

- What kinds of characters do we meet?
- What are the main characters like? How are they described?
- What typical events seem to happen?
- Are there similarities in the kinds of problems characters encounter? Are there similarities in the way the stories end?
- Where are the stories set? What similarities are there in the settings?
- Are there any common 'big ideas' the stories seem to be about?

You can set about exploring these questions in a variety of ways. You may retell some stories and read others aloud, and then encourage children to read these and two or three more they select for themselves through a reading contract you've drawn up. Charts for listing observations will help children to begin to make their comparisons — at a basic level they can be drawn on butcher's paper like this:

TASKS HEROES HAD TO PERFORM

Perseus	get the Gorgon's head
Theseus	kill the Minotaur
Jason	bring back the Golden Fleece

Attribute grids or charts of character traits are another way of teasing out information about characters. If different children complete them for characters from different stories, they can then work as a group to puzzle out similarities and differences. Of course, at the same time as they are undertaking this analysis, you can negotiate with them some of the other activities already suggested.

As a culmination to the study you might engage the class in drawing up a 'story retrieval' wall grid, with one axis listing the characteristics you have noted for the genre and the other the stories read. Children who have read particular stories can then fill in the cells of the grid.

From a study of Greek hero stories children might conclude that all the heroes have to undertake some kind of journey involving difficult tasks or trials, that they have particular strengths and weaknesses, and that they have the help of some supernatural being or artefact. In his introduction to *The Great Deeds of Superheroes* Maurice Saxby has created a comprehensive chart of this kind. His headings include 'hero', 'weapon or talisman', 'prophecy', 'tutor/mentor', 'tasks and trials', 'journey', 'strengths' and 'weaknesses'.

A thematic study
A variant on the genre study is to use myths and legends with other literature and other media to explore a more general theme, such as 'What is a hero?' Are there similarities, for example, between some of the Greek stories and those about Indiana Jones, or the *Star Wars* trilogy? Why do we need heroes? What is heroism in real life? Can each of us be a hero in one way or another? The last two questions might extend the theme to include the reading of some contemporary realistic fiction. In what ways can their major characters be described as heroic? Do they have journeys or quests to make? What are their tasks and trials? What 'monsters' must they confront?

A close study of story variants
Closely reading and comparing two (or preferably three or four) different retellings of a myth or legend can be a very interesting small group activity. Children become more aware of the variable tradition of storytelling in which the stories developed, and they also gain more awareness of the choices authors make in writing a story.

If there are enough versions to go round, each child in a group can read a different one, or children can work in pairs, each pair reading two versions. Beginning with the broad question 'In what ways do these stories differ?', ask the children to act as detectives, looking for differences in what the authors tell them. Your analysis might focus first on the 'content' of the story — the setting, sequence of events and the characters. Take, for example, the well-known story of King Midas: two versions differ in their accounts of what objects he turns to gold. In one they are objects from nature — a branch, a pebble, an apple and so on. In the other they are man-made objects within the palace — a chair, a table, drinking vessels . . . In the first version Midas embraces his children, with tragic consequences. In the second he is simply unhappy because he knows he dare not touch them. These and other differences might be listed in grid form.

The next and more important step is to examine how differences in the *telling* of the story may affect a reader's interpretation. For example, do the different items Midas turns to gold give the reader different impressions of him? In the first version he seems to be fairly innocently and haphazardly trying out a new 'skill', while in the second he is deliberately turning to gold all his material possessions. Does the first version, in which Midas turns his children to gold, create more drama than the second, where he seems doomed to keep them at arm's length?

You can also direct children's attention to other features of the retellings. Which version most impresses upon us Midas' greed? How are we told Midas is greedy? (Compare the wording in the two versions.) Do the authors *show* us this greed through action or dialogue? Which version is most sympathetic to Midas? Which do readers think concludes the story most satisfactorily? Do readers see the story differently in a version which explicitly draws a moral?

Conclusion

Through this kind of analysis children become aware that the impact of a story can be radically affected by what events are included, by the way they are presented and by myriad choices of wording. One root stock of traditional story can sprout many variants, and myths and legends allow us to see the process at work particularly clearly.

Another advantage of a genre or thematic study is that it takes us past our initial pleasure in the stories to question what they mean to us. I indicated in the introduction to this book that myths and legends form an enormous reservoir of reflection on human experience in narrative form. As such they continue to nourish our imaginations and understandings, and many children will find that characters and images they have encountered in the world's mythologies will lodge in their memories as reference points for the rest of their lives.

SELECT BIBLIOGRAPHY

The books listed here represent a selection of what is currently available from libraries and resource centres. They have been selected on the assumption that the teacher will engage as much in storytelling as in story reading. This means that I have included a wider range than would be the case if I had listed just those books which can be read aloud to children.

Over the past two or three decades publishers' interest in myths and legends seems to have declined. For example, in the early 1960s Oxford had in print a series of some fifteen hardback books of myths and legends from different cultures; currently only about five of these are available (in paperback). I would like to feel that the others will be reissued soon. In some areas, however, there has been an increase in interest — notably in Aboriginal Australian myths and legends. None the less, since the general trend for publishing myths and legends has weakened, teachers will probably have to make use of library services to obtain books they need; quite a number will be out of print.

The bibliography is arranged in several sections so that teachers can more easily look for suitable books to use in a chosen area, such as Norse mythology. Apart from the titles listed in the first section, I have included comments about all books (except picture books) to indicate their usefulness, and I have added the Dewey number to make them easier to find in libraries. I would expect that those books classified as 'Reference' will generally be consulted by teachers rather than children.

Books for the Teacher

Baker, A. & Greene, E. 1977, *Storytelling: Art and Technique*, Bowker, New York.

Bauer, C. F. 1977, *Handbook for Storytellers*, American Library Association, Chicago.

Chambers, A. 1992, *The Reading Environment*, PETA/Thimble Press, Sydney.

Colwell, E. 1980, *Storytelling*, Bodley Head, London.

Ellis, G. & Brewster, J. 1991, *The Storytelling Handbook for Primary Teachers*, Penguin, London.

Fox, M. 1980, *Thereby Hangs a Tale: A Storytelling How To*, Sturt College of Advanced Education, Adelaide.

Jennings, C. 1991, *Children as Story-tellers*, Oxford University Press, Melbourne.

Johnson, T. D. & Louis, D. R. 1985, *Literacy through Literature*, Nelson, Melbourne.

Livo, N. & Rietz, S. 1986, *Storytelling: Process and Practice*, Libraries Unlimited, Littleton, Colorado.

MacDonald, M. R. 1982, *The Storyteller's Sourcebook*, Gale Research, Detroit, Michigan.

Mallan, K. (ed.) 1990, *Telling Tales: A Sourcebook of Storytelling Ideas*, Queensland University of Technology, Brisbane.

Mallan, K. 1991, *Children as Storytellers*, PETA, Sydney.

Morgan, J. & Rinvolucri, M. 1983, *Once Upon a Time: Using Stories in the Language Classroom*, Cambridge University Press, Cambridge.

O'Sullivan, C. 1984, 'Fifteen Ways around a Traditional Tale', Reading Around Series, no. 3, Australian Reading Association, Melbourne.

Robertson, M. E. 1990, 'True Wizardry: Readers Theatre in the Classroom', PEN 79, PETA, Sydney.

Saxby, M. (ed.) 1979, *Through Folklore to Literature*, International Board on Books for Young People, Sydney.

Saxby, M. & Winch, G. 1987, *Give Them Wings: The Experience of Children's Literature*, Macmillan, Melbourne.

Sloan, P. & Latham, R. 1981, *Teaching Reading Is* . . . , Nelson, Melbourne.

Tasmanian Speech and Drama Centre 1980, *A Framework for Speech and Drama*, 5 booklets, Tasmania Media Centre, Hobart.

Walshe, R. D., Jensen, D. & Moore, T. (eds) 1983, *Teaching Literature*, PETA & English Teaching Association of NSW, Sydney.

General Mythology

The books listed in this section refer to mythologies from many different cultures. While some are concerned with a specific kind of myth (e.g. creation myths), most are reference books for the teacher to consult as needed. Generally they are not just collections of stories.

Bailey, J., McLeish, K. & Spearman, D. 1981, *Gods and Men: Myths and Legends from the World's Religions*, Oxford University Press, Oxford. § Reference; teacher retell. A useful collection of stories, but the language is too advanced for reading in the primary school. 398.2.

Cook, E. 1976, *The Ordinary and the Fabulous*, Cambridge University Press, Cambridge. § Reference. A perceptive book about the place of myths, legends and fairy tales in the classroom. It covers the secondary area as well as the primary school. A little out of date now, but still a very valuable reference for teachers. 028.5.

Eliot, A. 1976, *Myths*, McGraw-Hill, Maidenhead, Berks. § Reference. A very useful reference book containing brief versions of many different stories, arranged thematically. Also includes many illustrations and rather erudite chapters from mythographers Mercea Eliade and Joseph Campbell. 291.13.

Evans, C. & Millard, A. 1987, *Usborne Book of Greek and Norse Legends*, Usborne, London. § Reference. With brief retellings of the main stories, this is very much a reference book for teachers or older readers. Includes source charts, pronunciation guides, maps and a *who's who* section on characters in the stories. 398.22.

Farmer, P. 1979, *Beginnings: Creation Myths of the World*, Atheneum, New York. § Teacher read and retell. A collection of short myths (some only three lines long) about how things came into being. Drawn from many cultures, they are arranged under seven headings, such as 'Man' and 'Flood'. 398.22.

Grimal, P. 1965, *Larousse World Mythology*, Hamlyn, London. § Reference. A weighty volume, lavishly illustrated; one of the popular Larousse series of encyclopaedias. It is stronger in discussing the mythologies of different cultures than in giving stories which can be retold. 291.13.

Horowitz, A. 1985, *Kingfisher Book of Myths and Legends*, Kingfisher, London. § Teacher read and retell; upper primary pupil read. Famous stories from a wide range of ancient cultures, including Egypt, Babylon, Greece and India, retold quite simply. 398.22.

Ions, V. 1974, *The World's Mythology in Colour*, Hamlyn, London. § Reference. A well-illustrated book which gives much background information about the settings for myths and legends. 291.13.

Kirk, G. S. 1970, *Myth: Its Meaning and Functions in Ancient and Other Cultures*, Cambridge University Press, London. § Ultra reference. An erudite book for the real enthusiast. 291.13.

Leeming, D. A. 1981, *Mythology: The Voyage of the Hero*, Harper & Row, New York. § Teacher retell. A collection of myths and legends from different cultures arranged in subject groups; each group concludes with a commentary. Every myth or legend has been taken from an already published source. 291.13.

Rosenberg, D. & Baker, S. 1981, *Mythology and You*, National Textbook Co., Skokie, Illinois. § Reference; teacher retell. Mythological selections, commentary and study questions form the basis of this upper secondary textbook. There is a companion teacher's guide. 292.13.

Saxby, M. 1989, *The Great Deeds of Superheroes*, Millennium, Sydney. § Teacher read and retell; upper primary pupil read. Begins with an informative introduction and a chart of the heroes' characteristics. The stories, retold in scholarly style, are from the Greek, Norse, Old Testament and Mediaeval traditions. Strikingly illustrated by Robert Ingpen. 398.22.

Saxby, M. 1990, *The Great Deeds of Heroic Women*, Millennium, Sydney. § Teacher read and retell; upper primary pupil read. A companion volume to the above, again finely illustrated by Ingpen. Includes a Chinese goddess and some saints — a more varied collection than the male heroes. 398.22.

Stewart, M. 1987, *Creation Myths*, Southern Cross Reading Scheme, Macmillan, Melbourne. § Lower primary pupil read. 291.24.

Time-Life 1985, *Giants and Ogres*, Time-Life, Amsterdam. § Teacher read and retell; upper primary pupil read. One of a lavishly illustrated series of twenty-one books, entitled 'The Enchanted World', which covers folk tales as well as myths and legends. The text is suitable for older primary pupils, but the stories work well if the teacher reads or retells them. Very useful for a thematic approach. 398.21.

Greek Mythology

Our versions of Greek myths and legends derive from what was arguably the most literary culture in the ancient world, which continued to develop them over centuries after they were first written down. Greek mythology penetrated and transformed Roman mythology and was later to become a key element in forming the character of modern European culture. For some four hundred years the ascendancy of the study of the classical languages in English education ensured the continuing dissemination of Greek myths and legends — a process which has only been arrested this century. It is thus not surprising that many versions are readily available in libraries, ranging from translations of the original texts to compilations and retellings suitable for all levels in the primary school (and beyond). Nor is it surprising, given the long and complex history of the transmission of the stories, that considerable variation may be found between different versions.

Anderson, L. 1978, *Arion and the Dolphins*, Scribner, New York. § Picture book. 398.20938.

Barker, C. 1972, *King Midas and the Golden Touch*, Frank Watts, New York. § Picture book. 398.22.

Birrer, C. F. & W. 1987, *Song to Demeter*, Julia MacRea, London. § Picture book. 398.20938.

Church, A. J. 1964, *The Iliad and the Odyssey of Homer*, Macmillan, New York. § Teacher retell. These versions of the two Homeric epics, dating from the early years of this century, were written for children of upper primary age but are now best retold as the language may seem a little archaic. The structure is episodic; the chapters are short and thus ideal for adapting to classroom use. A few rather romantic line drawings are included. 398.20938.

Farmer, P. & Connor, C. 1971, *Daedalus and Icarus*, Collins, London. § Picture book. 398.20938.

Farmer, P. & Connor, C. 1971, *The Serpent's Teeth: The Story of Cadmus*, Collins, London. § Picture book. 398.20938.

Farmer, P. & McCallum, G. 1972, *The Story of Persephone*, Collins, London. § Picture book. 398.20938.

Farmer, P. & McCallum, G. 1975, *Heracles*, Collins, London. § Picture book. 398.20938.

Gibson, M. 1978, *Gods, Men and Monsters from the Greek Myths*, Hodder, Sydney. § Reference; teacher retell. A compilation of stories about individual gods, goddesses, heroes and monsters (e.g. Theseus and the Minotaur). There are many colourful illustrations and line drawings. The text could be read aloud but is probably better used as a source for retellings in the classroom, as the language may be a little advanced for most primary school pupils. 398.20938.

Grant, M. 1962, *Myths of the Greeks and Romans*, Mentor, New York. § Reference. Although most of the Greek myths are included, they are interspersed with comment and so it is not always easy to find a particular story. The illustrations, maps and genealogy tables can be useful. 292.

Graves, R. 1981, *Greek Myths*, illustrated edition, Penguin, London. § Reference; teacher retell. Abbreviated and illustrated version of Graves' earlier two-volume work, *The Greek Myths*. Better as a story source book for teachers than the two-volume set, which would be regarded as reference only. 398.20938.

Green, R. L. 1960, *Heroes of Greece and Troy*, Bodley Head, London. § Teacher read and retell; upper primary pupil read. This collection of stories was originally published by Puffin as two separate books, *Tales of the Greek Heroes* and *The Tale of Troy*. The first section deals with Perseus, Theseus, the Argonauts and Heracles; the second with Troy. The stories are well told and relatively short, and most upper primary children will find them easy to read. 398.20938.

Green, R. L. 1961, *The Luck of Troy*, Puffin, Harmondsworth, Middlesex. § Teacher read and retell; upper primary pupil read. The author uses the Homeric account of the Trojan war but supplies an authentic background from other sources. Well told in a lively style, this is a very useful book for reading to Years 5–7 in the primary school. 292.21.

Green, R. L. 1977, *The Tale of Thebes*, Cambridge University Press, London. § Teacher read and retell; upper primary pupil read. A collection of ten stories revolving around the city of Thebes and its influence in the classical Greek world. Some, such as the story of Oedipus, are better known than others. Since the author establishes a context at the beginning of each story, there is often some overlapping detail which the teacher will want to omit in retelling. Two useful maps and a Theban royal family tree are included. 398.20938.

Grimal, P. 1986, *The Dictionary of Classical Mythology*, Blackwell, Oxford. § Reference. In addition to its entries for mythological characters, this volume contains a list of sources for various myths and legends and a set of genealogical tables. 292.1.

Guirands, F. 1963, *Greek Mythology*, Hamlyn, London. § Reference. A useful reference book which deals briefly with most aspects of Greek mythology in an orderly and scholarly manner. Covers the gods who live on Mt Olympus, the origins of natural phenomena such as the sun and the sea, and finally stories of the heroes. Middle and upper primary pupils will enjoy the illustrations. 292.08.

Kerenyi, C. 1979, *The Gods of the Greeks*, Thames & Hudson, London. § Reference. An academic work which deals with the Greek divinities and some of the mythological creatures, such as centaurs and satyrs, but not with the heroes or with the Trojan war. It is not particularly easy to read (the language is rather stilted), but it can be used to fill in details that may have been omitted from other books, or to find alternative versions of stories. 292.13.

Kirk, G. S. 1975, *The Nature of Greek Myths*, Overlook Press, Woodstock, New York. § Ultra reference. A scholarly book covering different interpretations of Greek myths, with important comments about the gods and heroes. 292.13.

Lang, A. 1972, *The Adventures of Odysseus*, Dent, London. § Teacher retell. A classic version, dating from the early years of this century, which incorporates in the stories the social conditions and conventions prevailing at the time of the Trojan war. The language will need a little adapting, but the authenticity of the stories makes this still a worthwhile book. 398.20938.

Mackenzie, C. 1968, *The Strongest Man on Earth*, Chatto & Windus, London. § Teacher read and retell; middle/upper primary pupil read. Includes the stories of the twelve labours of Heracles, together with brief accounts of his birth and some of his other adventures, such as his joining Jason and the Argonauts. Related in an easy-going style, this collection was put together after the author's earlier broadcast work on Theseus. Good for reading both to and by pupils in the middle/upper primary school. 292.211.

MacKenzie, C. 1970, *Perseus*, Aldus, London. § Teacher read and retell; middle/upper primary pupil read. 398.20938.

MacKenzie, C. 1972, *Achilles*, Aldus, London. § Teacher read and retell; middle/upper primary pupil read. 398.20938.

MacKenzie, C. 1972, *Jason*, Aldus, London. § Teacher read and retell; middle/upper primary pupil read. 398.20938.

MacKenzie, C. 1972, *Theseus*, Aldus, London. § Teacher read and retell; middle/upper primary pupil read. 398.20938.

Morford, M. P. O. & Lenardon, R. J. 1977, *Classical Mythology*, Longman, New York. § Reference; teacher retell. Intended for an undergraduate audience, this covers the major creation myths and the sagas of the heroes (including Perseus, Heracles and the Argonauts), as well as stories associated with places such as Troy, Thebes and Mycenae. Also contains some useful maps and family trees. 292.13.

Patrick, R. 1972, *The All Colour Book of Greek Mythology*, Octopus, London. § Reference. Deals with the history and nature of Greek myths and attempts a distinction between myth and folktale, but does not actually tell the stories. Much of the book is given over to a superb collection of myth-inspired Greek art, which can be shared with children; each illustration is accompanied by an explanatory text. 292.08.

Pinsent, J. 1969, *Greek Mythology*, Hamlyn, London. § Reference. A scholarly examination of what constitutes mythology with a history of the different forms of stories, both familiar and less familiar. Psychological and philosophical backgrounds to stories are given too. The book is beautifully illustrated, and although the pictures will be appreciated by children, the text is for the enthusiastic and persevering teacher. 292.08.

Reeves, J. 1973, *The Voyage of Odysseus*, Blackie, Glasgow. § Teacher read and retell; upper primary pupil read. A detailed, well-written account of the wanderings of Odysseus; the language is slightly old-fashioned but not difficult to understand. There is a helpful map and a pronunciation guide at the beginning. 398.20938.

Serraillier, I. 1971, *Heracles the Strong*, Hamish Hamilton, London. § Teacher read and retell; upper primary pupil read. A fine retelling of the stories of Heracles from his birth to his death, illustrated with line drawings. Easily read by upper primary pupils and good for reading as well as retelling by teachers.

Swinburne, L. & I. 1977, *Ancient Myths: The First Science Fiction*, Contemporary Perspectives, New York. § Middle primary pupil read. A set of four stories about Heracles, Perseus, Orpheus and Achilles, written under the assumption that they parallel contemporary comic-strip heroes (e.g. Batman or Superman). 292.13.

Warner, R. 1950, *Men and Gods*, Heinemann, London. § Teacher read and retell; upper primary pupil read. A wide selection of Greek stories, authentic and well told without embroidery, though occasionally there is a slip in the use of a Roman name (e.g. Ceres) among the Greek ones. 292.211.

Warner, R. 1952, *Greeks and Trojans*, Heinemann, London. § Teacher read and retell; upper primary pupil read. A useful adaptation of some stories from the *Iliad*, despite there seeming to be more listing of names than real storytelling in places. Helpful in creating a context for drama. 292.211.

Warner, R. 1969, *The Vengeance of the Gods*, Heinemann, London. § Teacher read and retell; upper primary pupil read. A telling of nine stories which are almost independent of each other. They include four about Agamemnon, Iphigenia and Orestes, the story of Prometheus, and the story of Alcestis and her rescue from the underworld by the ever-obliging Heracles. Very useful for the teacher to both read and retell to middle and upper primary pupils. 292.211.

Northern European Mythology

This section includes Norse or Viking myths and legends (e.g. stories about Thor and Odin, Loki and Baldur), Germanic ones (e.g. stories about Siegfried), Celtic ones (e.g. stories about King Arthur or Finn Mac Cool) and Anglo-Saxon ones (e.g. stories about Beowulf). They can be grouped together thematically as well as geographically. For example, they tend to set a high value on bravery, especially courage in battle — an emphasis later refined in the chivalric themes of the Arthurian cycle. Some stories, entirely pagan in origin, were modified by the influence of Christianity, which was widely dispersed by the time they were written down.

Asbjornsen, P. C. & Moe, T. C. 1963, *East of the Sun and West of the Moon*, Macmillan, New York. § Teacher read and retell; middle/upper primary pupil read. A collection of traditional tales from Norway. 398.2.

Baldwin, J. 1959, *The Story of Siegfried*, Scribner, New York. § Teacher retell. First published more than sixty years ago, these stories about Siegfried are well narrated and accompanied by illustrations and brief notes. However, they must be retold as the language will appear antique to most children. 398.20943.

Boucher, A. 1967, *Stories of the Norsemen*, Burke, London. § Teacher read and retell; upper primary pupil read. A useful retelling of Viking stories in a language suitable for older children. Includes the *Volsung Saga*. 398.20948.

Bowen, O. 1959, *Tales from the Mabinogion*, Vanguard Press, New York. § Teacher retell. An illustrated version of the eleven mediaeval Welsh prose stories collectively called *The Mabinogion*. Includes notes on the pronunciation of Welsh names. The language is such that a retelling will be better than a reading for most primary school children. 398.209429.

Branston, B. 1978, *Gods and Heroes from Viking Mythology*, Hodder, Sydney. § Teacher read and retell; upper primary pupil read. This book contains most of the important stories from the Norse myths, told within the frame of an investigation by Gylfi, an old Swedish king. It is well illustrated with both colour and line drawings by Giovanni Caselli. The language may need simplifying if read to middle primary children. 293.211.

Crossley-Holland, K. 1977, *The Faber Book of Northern Legends*, Faber, London. § Teacher read and retell; upper primary pupil read. A good collection of some of the northern myths. There are four parts: the first deals with the Norse gods; the second with heroes of the Germanic legends; the third includes some of the Icelandic sagas, and the final part ('Twilight of the Gods') returns to the Norse myths and covers the later events leading up to Ragnarok. 398.2.

Crossley-Holland, K. 1980, *The Norse Myths*, Andre Deutsch, London. § Teacher read and retell. Thirty-two dramatic narratives about the Norse gods and heroes — a comprehensive retelling of the myths from creation to Ragnarok. Has a very useful introduction and glossary of names, as well as a bibliography which includes the sources. A good book for the teacher to read or use as a basis for retelling, but a little too difficult for primary school pupils to read on their own. 398.20948.

Crossley-Holland, K. 1984, *Beowulf*, Oxford University Press, Oxford. § Teacher read and retell. Dramatic, violent illustrations by Charles Keeping match the text in this fine version, which will appeal to older children. 398.23.

D'Aulaire, I. & E. 1967, *Norse Gods and Giants*, Doubleday, New York. § Teacher read and retell; upper primary pupil read. A well-illustrated version of the Norse myths, suitable for reading to middle and upper primary pupils. The brief chapters or episodes can be linked to form a longer narrative. Includes a useful glossary of names with helpful pronunciation suggestions. 293.211.

Davidson, H. R. E. 1982, *Scandinavian Mythology*, Hamlyn, London. § Reference; teacher retell. An illustrated book from an expert in the area, part of the 'Library of the World's Myths and Legends' (there were some eighteen volumes in the series). Contains both myths and legends, as well as having some sections devoted to the religion underlying the mythology. 293.1.

Feagles, A. M. 1968, *Thor and the Giants*, Young Scott, New York. § Teacher read and retell; middle primary pupil read. A retelling of one of the adventures of Thor, copiously illustrated. Useful with younger pupils. 293.

Gantz, G. 1976, *The Mabinogion*, Penguin, Harmondsworth, Middlesex. § Reference; teacher retell. The 'standard' version of the famous collection of Welsh legends, best used as a resource for finding out about one of these stories, rather than as a book of tales to be read to a class. 398.209429.

Grant, J. 1990, *An Introduction to Viking Mythology*, Apple Press, London. § Reference; teacher read and retell; upper primary pupil read. Starts with a useful glossary containing many long entries about characters and places not given story treatment in the succeeding pages. The stories are interesting in themselves but the selection is restricted. 293.

Green, R. L. 1970, *Myths of the Norsemen*, Puffin, Harmondsworth, Middlesex. § Teacher read and retell; upper primary pupil read. Originally published as *The Saga of Asgard*, this book contains an excellent retelling of the myths and legends of the Viking era. A very good source for the stories from the creation to the final battle of Ragnarok. 398.209363.

Jones, G. 1975, *Welsh Legends and Folk Tales*, Oxford University Press, London. § Teacher read and retell; upper primary pupil read. An easy-to-read version of the Welsh tales known as *The Mabinogion* and others from the Arthurian era. Includes some good illustrations by Joan Kiddell-Monroe. 398.209429.

Keary, A. & E. 1976, *The Heroes of Asgard*, Core Collection Books, New York. § Teacher retell. This book is a reprint of an 1870 publication. There are a few drawings, not very clear, but the text is useful as a source for retellings. 398.20948.

MacCana, P. 1970, *Celtic Mythology*, Hamlyn, London. § Reference. An illustrated book which gives the background to the Irish section of Celtic mythology. Although there are references to the stories, little of their body gets into the text: for example, there is some background to the stories of Fionn mac Cumhaill (Finn Mac Cool), but you won't find out why he built the Giants Causeway. 299.16.

Perham, M. 1993, *King Arthur and the Legends of Camelot*, Dragon's World, Limpsfield, Surrey. § Teacher read and retell. A detailed retelling of all the main Arthurian stories in a lavish gift book with many illustrations by Julek Heller. 398.23.

Sutcliff, R. 1961, *Beowulf: Dragon Slayer*, Bodley Head, London. § Teacher read and retell; upper primary pupil read. An excellent retelling of the Old English story of Beowulf. There are a few line drawings to help give interest, but the real interest will come from a reading of the superb text. 398.22.

Sutcliff, R. 1967, *The High Deeds of Finn Mac Cool*, Penguin, Harmondsworth, Middlesex. § Teacher read and retell; upper primary pupil read. Story of the Irish hero Finn Mac Cool told as a historical novel. Can be read to both middle and upper primary school pupils, but may need some selecting and adapting when used with the younger group. Not so much a myth/legend book but a tale of a folk hero. 398.22.

Sutcliff, R. 1971, *Tristan and Iseult*, Bodley Head, London. § Teacher read and retell; upper primary pupil read. A version of the story of Tristan and Isolde without the love-potion. This is an excellent retelling set out in short chapters — a pattern which can be followed when it's read to a class. 398.22.

Sutcliff, R. 1979, *The Light beyond the Forest*, Bodley Head, London. § Teacher read and retell; upper primary pupil read. The search for the

Holy Grail, lyrically told by this distinguished historical writer. Her Arthurian cycle was completed in 1981 with the publication of *The Sword and the Circle* (Arthur's early days) and *The Road to Camlann* (Arthur's death), which are equally recommendable. 398.23.

Thomas, G. & Crossley-Holland, K. 1984, *Tales from the Mabinogion*, Gollancz, London. § Teacher read and retell; upper primary pupil read. Commissioned by the Welsh Arts Council and illustrated by Margaret Jones, this is an account of the four 'branches' of the *Mabinogion* in vivid language with plenty of dialogue. 398.35.

Turner, B. 1992, *Beowulf's Downfall*, Harcourt Brace, Sydney. § Teacher read and retell; upper primary pupil read. Covers the period of Scandinavian history in which Beowulf figured and his last, fatal battle with the dragon, but not his encounters with Grendel and Grendel's mother. Atmospheric illustrations by the author. 398.22.

Wilson, B. K. 1989, *Scottish Folk Tales and Legends*, Oxford University Press, London. § Teacher read and retell; upper primary pupil read. A collection of over thirty stories from Scotland. This is a recent reissue in paperback of one of a series featuring stories from different parts of the world. Nearer a collection of folk tales than legends, it has many eminently readable stories for middle and upper primary children. 398.20942.

Australian Aboriginal Lore

'Lore' is the term used by many Australian Aboriginals in preference to mythology, myth or legend. The stories available to us from the diversity of Australian Aboriginal cultures are generally shorter and less interconnected than, say, those from the Greek or Norse mythologies. Thus they are often more accessible to children lower down in the primary school. They are also less developed in a literary sense because they still exist within an oral tradition — in fact the currency of their oral nature gives them a very distinctive importance. If you live in a part of Australia where liaison with Aboriginal groups makes possible storytelling visits to or by members of a local tribe, it's very much worthwhile arranging one.

N.B. *The Dewey classification number has been omitted from individual entries in this section because it is the same for all books listed: viz 398.20994.*

Barlow, A. 1991, *The Brothers Barmbarmbutt and Mopoke*, Southern Cross Reading Scheme, Macmillan, Melbourne. § Picture book. Other picture books by the same author, published in the same year and series, include:
> *Gurangatch and Mirraga*
> *How Kaaloo Set the Waters Flowing*
> *Kuboro the Koala*
> *Red Tit and Brown Tit*
> *Why Brolga Has Only Two Chicks.*

Berndt, C. 1979, *Land of the Rainbow Snake*, Collins, Sydney. § Teacher read and retell; middle/upper primary pupil read. A collection of stories from western Arnhem Land, delightfully illustrated with line drawings. In addition there are fifteen songs printed in both Gunwinggu and English. Many of these songs are linked to a specific place where something special happened; the stories tell what that special event was.

Berndt, C. 1987, *Pheasant and Kingfisher*, Ashton, Gosford. § Teacher read and retell; middle/upper primary pupil read. A set of stories originally told by Nganalgindia in the Gunwinggu language. Fine colour illustrations by Raymond Meeks.

Brunato, M. 1975, *Worra and Legends of the Booandiks*, Rigby, Perth. § Picture book.

Chek, C. H. 1976, *The Flower Seekers*, Federal Publications, Singapore. § Picture book.

Djugurba: Tales from the Spirit Time 1974, ANU Press, Canberra. § Teacher read; middle/upper primary pupil read. Young Aboriginal students training as teachers at Kormilda College, Darwin, wrote and illustrated this book cooperatively. The origin stories are simply told and are suitable for reading even to the very young.

Fox, N. K. 1979, *Tjuma: Stories from the Western Desert*, Aboriginal Board of the Arts Council of Australia, Canberra. § Picture book.

Gordon, T. & Haviland, J. B. 1979, *Milbi: Aboriginal Tales from Queensland's Endeavour River*, ANU Press, Canberra. § Picture book.

Greene, G., Tramacchi, J. & Gill, L. 1992, *Tjarany Roughtail*, Magabala, Broome. § Teacher read; middle/upper primary pupil read. Bilingual text in Kukatja and English of traditional stories, illustrated in colour. Includes language lists, pronunciation guide and kinship diagrams — a book to pore over.

Gulpilil 1979, *Gulpilil's Stories of the Dreamtime*, Collins, Sydney. § Teacher read and retell; upper primary pupil read. Generously illustrated with photographs, this book derives from films made by the author.

Lawrie, M. 1970, *Myths and Legends of Torres Strait*, University of Queensland Press, Brisbane. § Teacher read and retell; upper primary pupil read. A substantial collection of stories from the Torres Strait region. All the stories are told by islanders and have been faithfully translated from the original language. The book is well illustrated and there are informative notes. An excellent collection.

Lofts, P. 1983, *Dunbi the Owl*, Ashton, Gosford. § Picture book.

Lofts, P. 1983, *How the Birds Got Their Colours*, Ashton, Gosford. § Picture book.

Lofts, P. 1984, *The Echidna and the Shade Tree*, Ashton, Gosford. § Picture book.

Marawili, W. 1977, *Djet*, Nelson, Melbourne. § Picture book. Has the Aboriginal text and an English translation.

Mountford, C. P. 1973, *The Dreamtime Book*, Nelson, Melbourne. § Teacher read and retell; upper primary pupil read. One of several collections of Aboriginal stories made by Mountford, this book has illustrations from bark paintings and finger paintings by members of Tiwi, Pitjantjara and Junkanjara tribes. It contains a selection of seventy-nine stories first published in *The Dreamtime* (1956), *The Dawn of Time* (1968) and *The First Sunrise* (1971), all of which were illustrated by Ainslie Roberts. The stories can be useful in the classroom, but it must be borne in mind that they are very much versions of their time, told by the 'whitefella'.

Nangan, J. & Edwards, H. 1976, *Joe Nangan's Dreaming*, Nelson, Melbourne. § Teacher read; middle/upper primary pupil read. An illustrated book of stories from north-west Australia.

Noonuccal, O. 1990, *Legends of Our Land*, Harcourt Brace, Sydney. § Teacher read and retell; upper primary pupil read. Contains two stories each from Stradbroke Island, Western Australia and Tasmania. Illustrated with landscape photographs and the author's drawings.

Noonuccal, O. 1992, *Australia's Unwritten History: More Legends of Our Land*, Harcourt Brace, Sydney. § Teacher read and retell; upper primary pupil read. A sequel to the above.

Nunes, S. 1989, *Tiddalick the Frog*, Hodder, Sevenoaks, Kent. § Picture book.

Parker, K. L. 1969, *Australian Legendary Tales*, Rigby, Adelaide. § Teacher read and retell; upper primary pupil read. A reissue of one of the earliest published collections of Aboriginal stories, made by Mrs Parker at the end of the nineteenth century. Includes a glossary of Aboriginal words.

Reed, A. W. 1965, *Aboriginal Fables*, Reed, Sydney. § Teacher read and retell; upper primary pupil read. A collection of over seventy 'just so' stories — good for retelling in the lower primary school.

Reed, A. W. 1965, *Myths and Legends of Australia*, Reed, Sydney. § Teacher read and retell; upper primary pupil read. A collection of Aboriginal stories organised under themes such as creation, animals, etc. Useful, but the style of retelling is rather European.

Robinson, R. 1956, *The Feathered Serpent*, Edwards and Shaw, Sydney. § Teacher read; upper primary pupil read. Robinson recorded tales told by Aboriginal tribal elders, and they are published here in the language of the tellers. Authentic and valuable in primary schools.

Robinson, R. 1967, *Legend and Dreaming*, Edwards and Shaw, Sydney. § Teacher read and retell; upper primary pupil read. Here Robinson followed the same procedure as in his earlier book, and the result, illustrated by the narrators, is equally valuable.

Roennfeldt, R. 1980, *Tiddalick: The Frog Who Caused a Flood*, Puffin, Ringwood. § Picture book.

Roughsey, D. 1973, *The Giant Devil-Dingo*, Collins, Sydney. § Picture book.

Roughsey, D. 1975, *The Rainbow Serpent*, Collins, Sydney. § Picture book.

Stevens, T. 1983, *The Lost Boomerang*, Methuen, Sydney. § Picture book.

Thomas, W. J. (n.d.), *Some Myths and Legends of Australian Aborigines*, Collins, Melbourne. § Teacher retell. A booklet giving several stories which, like much Aboriginal lore, help to explain the strong links between the people and their environment. The few pictures are of dubious quality.

Timepatua, M. A. 1977, *Kwork Kwork*, ANU Press, Canberra. Teacher read and retell; upper primary pupil read. A successor to *Djugurba* (see above).

Torres, P. & Williams, M. 1987, *The Story of Crow*, Magabala, Broome. § Picture book.

Trezise, P. 1987, *The Owl People*, Collins, Sydney. § Picture book.

Trezise, P. & Roughsey, D. 1978, *The Quinkins*, Collins, Sydney. § Picture book.

Trezise, P. & Roughsey, D. 1982, *Turramulli and the Giant Quinkin*, Collins, Sydney. § Picture book.

Trezise, P. & Roughsey, D. 1983, *The Magic Firesticks*, Collins, Sydney. § Picture book.

Trezise, P. & Roughsey, D. 1984, *Gijda*, Collins, Sydney. § Picture book.

Utemorrah, D. 1980, *Visions of Mowanjum*, Rigby, Adelaide. § Teacher read; upper primary pupil read. A collection of stories from the Mowanjum people, a small community near Derby in the Kimberley district of Western Australia. Many of the stories are told by Daisy Utemorrah and Elkin Umbagai, who include some autobiographical material.

Walker, K. 1972, *Stradbroke Dreamtime*, Angus and Robertson, Sydney. § Teacher read; upper primary pupil read. Kath Walker, who was later to resume her Aboriginal name, Oodgeroo Noonuccal (see titles above), here includes tales from her childhood, as well as some which she describes as from 'the Old and New Dreamtime'.

Wells, A. E. 1973, *The Dew Wet Earth*, Rigby, Perth. § Teacher read; upper primary pupil read. An illustrated book of tales from Arnhem Land.

Weir, I. (n.d.), *Legends of the Aborigines*, 12 vols, Reed, Sydney. § Infant/lower primary pupil read. Valuable in providing texts accessible to younger readers.

Western Australian Education Department (n.d.), *Pictures That Talk*, Perth. § Picture book.

Wilson, B. K. 1972, *Tales Told to Kabbarli: Aboriginal Legends Collected by Daisy Bates*, Angus and Robertson, Sydney. § Teacher read and retell; middle/upper primary pupil read. These stories remained unpublished on Daisy Bates' death in 1951 and were prepared for press by Barbara Ker Wilson. They emphasise the strong connection between Australian Aborigines and their environment.

Myths and Legends of Other Peoples

This section contains a reasonable variety of books devoted to the myths and legends of cultures other than those of the Greek, Northern European and Australian Aboriginal peoples. Two versions of the epic of Gilgamesh, believed to be the oldest written story, are included, but generally there are few accessible myths from ancient civilisations such as the Egyptian and Aztec. (This may appear surprising when set against the range of buildings surviving from those civilisations.) We have more stories from cultures, such as the African, West Indian or Maori, where the oral tradition has either continued till recent times or is still alive today. Such stories have been recorded by anthropologists, as well as by those interested mainly in the stories themselves.

Alderson, B. 1992, *The Arabian Nights: Or Tales Told by Sheherezade during a Thousand Nights and One Night*, Gollancz, London. § Teacher read and retell. This lavish edition includes rich gilded illustrations by Michael Foreman, as well as useful notes on the stories' origins. The Sheherezade structure is retained, and there are some less familiar tales besides favourites like 'Sindbad the Sailor', 'Ali Baba' and 'Aladdin'. 398.32.

Anderson, V. 1979, *Sinabouda Lily: A Folk Tale from Papua New Guinea*, Oxford University Press, Melbourne. § Picture book. 398.20995.

Appiah, P. 1967, *Tales of an Ashanti Father*, Andre Deutsch, London. § Teacher read and retell; upper primary pupil read. Stories from Ghana collected for telling to children, particularly those from western societies. Excellent for reading and telling to middle and upper primary children. 398.209667.

Arnott, K. 1962, *African Myths and Legends*, Oxford University Press, London. § Teacher read and retell; upper primary pupil read. A collection of African myths and legends rather like the 'just so' stories from other lands. They come from most parts of Africa except the north. Useful for reading and telling to middle primary children. 398.2096.

Birch, C. 1961, *Chinese Myths and Fantasies*, Oxford University Press, Oxford. § Teacher read and retell; upper primary pupil read. Creation, the Flood, ghost stories and the Revolt of the Demons cycle are all told in fairly simple style. 398.32.

Bryson, B. (n.d.), *Gilgamesh*, Holt, Rinehart and Winston, New York. § Teacher read and retell; upper primary pupil read. A delightful version of the Sumerian epic which can be told or read in short sections as it appears here. The book is illustrated but the illustrations may not appeal to children. 398.22.

Buffet, G. & B. 1972, *Kama Pua'a*, Rigby, Adelaide. § Picture book. A Hawaiian story. 398.20996.

Buffet, G. & B. 1973, *Kahala*, Rigby, Adelaide. § Picture book. A Hawaiian story. 398.20996.

Dickinson, P. 1980, *City of Gold and Other Stories from the Old Testament*, Gollancz, London. § Teacher read and retell; upper primary pupil read. Jewish stories retold from the point of view of an observer or participant, such as a soldier or a priest. 221.950519.

Gray, J. E. B. 1961, *Indian Tales and Legends*, Oxford University Press, London. § Teacher read and retell; upper primary pupil read. Includes Buddha birth stories, animal stories and stories from the Ramayana and Mahabharata. 398.20934.

Hallworth, G. 1978, *Listen to This Story: Tales from the West Indies*, Magnet Books, London. § Teacher read and retell; upper primary pupil read. A book in a 'read aloud' series from a writer who grew up in Jamaica. Some Anansi (spider) stories are included, as well as a few lively illustrations and a brief glossary of West Indian words. 398.209729.

Jadfrey, M. & Foreman, M. 1985, *Seasons of Splendour: Tales, Myths and Legends of India*, Hodder, Sydney. § Teacher read and retell. Contains stories similar to those listed for Gray's book above. Could be read by the enthusiastic upper primary pupil, but is best used as a source book for the teacher. 398.20934.

Lane, S. 1973, *Maori Tales*, Penguin, Harmondsworth, Middlesex. § Middle primary pupil read. A very useful collection of Maori tales adapted as a set of playscripts for reading aloud. The various parts are graded in reading difficulty, and children can be given different parts as their reading proficiency increases. 398.220931.

Mataira, K. 1972, *Maui and the Big Fish*, Angus and Robertson, Sydney. § Picture book. A Maori story. 398.209931.

McDermott, G. 1977, *The Voyage of Osiris*, Windmill, New York. § Picture book. A story of ancient Egypt. 398.20932.

Mike, J. M. 1993, *Gift of the Nile: An Ancient Egyptian Legend*, Troll, USA. § Picture book. 398.32.

Newton Chocolate, D. M. 1993, *Spider and Sky God: An Akan Legend*, Troll, USA. § Picture book. An African story. 398.32.

Newton Chocolate, D. M. 1993, *Talk, Talk: An Ashanti Legend*, Troll, USA. § Picture book. A West African story. 398.32.

Poignant, R. 1967, *Oceanic Mythology: The Myths of Polynesia, Micronesia, Melanesia and Australia*, Hamlyn, London. § Teacher retell. Part of a series which includes Indian, Greek and Egyptian mythologies. This volume offers a wide-ranging collection of stories (though no Maori ones) and fills a gap in our knowledge of the mythology of our near neighbours in the south-west Pacific. Illustrated with superb photographs and paintings, which are more accessible to children than the text. 398.2099.

Reed, A. W. 1964, *Myths and Legends of Maoriland*, Reed, Wellington. § Teacher read and retell; upper primary pupil read. A valuable source book for many of the Maori myths and legends. Probably best retold, as the language reflects the original publication date of 1946. 398.220931.

Reed A.W. 1964, *The Wonder Book of Maori Legends*, Reed, Wellington. § Teacher read and retell; upper primary pupil read. A well-told set of stories about Maui, Rata and others, originally published under the title *Wonder Tales of Maoriland*. Includes simple line illustrations by A. S. Paterson. 398.2.

Roaul-Duval, F. 1971, *Pitali and Gurigo*, Collins, London. § Picture book. A South American Indian story. 398.2099.

Rockwell, A. 1971, *Tuhurahura and the Whale*, Parents' Magazine Press, New York. § Picture book. A Maori story. 398.209931.

Sherlock, P. 1966, *West Indian Folk Tales*, Oxford University Press, London. § Teacher read and retell. A useful collection of stories which includes some Anansi (spider) tales. 398.209729.

Wilson, B. K. & Stopkes, D. (eds) 1978, *The Turtle and the Island*, Hodder, Sydney. § Teacher read and retell; upper primary pupil read. A story from Papua New Guinea. 398.20995.

Zeman, L. 1992, *Gilgamesh the King*, Heinemann, London. § Teacher read; middle/upper primary pupil read. Very simple retelling and beautiful illustrations by this Czech artist. 398.32.